Other Books by James Montgomery Boice

Witness and Revelation in the Gospel of John
Philippians: An Expositional Commentary
The Sermon on the Mount
How to Really Live It Up
The Last and Future World
How God Can Use Nobodies
The Gospel of John: An Expositional Commentary (5 vols.)
"Galatians" in the *Expositor's Bible Commentary*
Can You Run Away from God?
Our Sovereign God, editor
The Sovereign God (Volume I of this series)
God the Redeemer (Volume II of this series)
The Foundation of Biblical Authority, editor

Foundations of the Christian Faith
VOLUME III

AWAKENING TO GOD

James Montgomery Boice

InterVarsity Press
Downers Grove
Illinois 60515

InterVarsity Press is the book-publishing division
of Inter-Varsity Christian Fellowship,
a student movement active on campus at hundreds
of universities, colleges and schools of nursing.
For information about local and regional
activities, write IVCF, 233 Langdon St.,
Madison, WI 53703.

Distributed in Canada through
InterVarsity Press, 1875 Leslie St., Unit 10,
Don Mills, Ontario M3B 2M5, Canada.

ISBN 0-87784-745-2

Library of Congress Catalog
Card Number: 78-25014

Printed in the United States of America

To him
who dwells with us
and is in us

Preface

If ever there was a generation that should respond to a Christian theology of the Holy Spirit's application of salvation to the self, it is this one. For in the latter half of the twentieth century we are preoccupied with the self, and this third volume of Foundations of the Christian Faith focuses on God's work in an individual.

This is not the whole of religion, as we have already seen and will continue to see. There are prior matters: the nature and attributes of God, the self-revelation of God to us in the Bible, the objective foundation for salvation in the work of Christ. There are matters that follow, among them the doctrine of the church and a Christian view of history. (When God saves a person, he does not save him in isolation. Rather, he brings the believer into a new, spiritual family in which the child of God thereafter enjoys new privileges and responsibilities.) These are suggested in this volume but are to be developed more fully in volume four.

The awakening of a man or woman to God is, nonetheless,

an important part of religion. For without this transforming experience, the doctrine of God is mere theory, the work of Christ just history, and the fellowship of the people of God a mere sociological oddity in which *we* have no part. In this volume, then, I first deal with the person and work of the Holy Spirit, next the application of grace to the individual, then the Christian life and finally the controversial subjects of election and perseverance.

This four-volume series follows the ground covered by John Calvin in his monumental *Institutes of the Christian Religion*. But this is not a rehash of the *Institutes*. What I have tried to do is cover the general areas of theology covered by Calvin but from a new perspective. I have eliminated many of those subjects that seemed important in his day but are less so in ours and introduced subjects that Calvin neglected but which are of major concern to us in the twentieth century. The clearest example of this is Calvin's neglect of any specific treatment of the attributes of God which occupied considerable space in volume one.

I am indebted to a number of other scholars most of whom are clearly identified in the footnotes. My biggest debt is to John Murray who has dealt with the work of the Holy Spirit brilliantly and concisely in *Redemption Accomplished and Applied*. Portions of this material have already appeared in some form in other places in my writings. These are indicated in the notes.

I wish to express appreciation to Miss Caecilie M. Foelster, my secretary, who assists in the production of all my books. I am also thankful for the evening congregation of Tenth Presbyterian Church in Philadelphia who first heard these messages in sermon form and responded with many valuable comments and suggestions.

May God be honored in the distribution and use of this book, and may it cause many to awake to him whose call is life eternal.

PART I
THE SPIRIT OF GOD

*You believe that God is one; you do well.
Even the demons believe—and shudder.
(Jas. 2:19)*

*"When the Spirit of truth comes, he will guide
you into all the truth; for he will not
speak on his own authority, but whatever he
hears he will speak, and he will declare
to you the things that are to come. He will
glorify me, for he will take what is mine
and declare it to you. All that the Father has
is mine; therefore I said that he will take
what is mine and declare it to you."
(Jn. 16:13-14)*

*I have been crucified with Christ; it is no
longer I who live, but Christ who lives
in me; and the life I now live in the flesh I live
by faith in the Son of God, who loved
me and gave himself for me. (Gal. 2:20)*

1 PERSONAL CHRISTIANITY

In Cathy's home her mother and father always spoke openly about spiritual things. The family went to church together, and Cathy attended Sunday school and various youth activities. When she was in high school she served on the planning committee of the High School Fellowship. So far as she knew she believed everything she had been taught. But then she went away to college, and as she began to be challenged by new ideas and to think through her faith, she slowly came to see that her early beliefs actually had little impact on her life. She once told me, "It's not that I am rejecting my parents' faith. I probably still believe it. It's just that it doesn't seem to mean anything to me personally. I'm not really sure I'm a Christian."

Mark, a young chemistry major, came from a non-Christian background. When he entered school, Christianity was the furthest thing from his mind. But he fell in with Christians from the very first day. They invited him to a weekly Friday night meeting. Between meetings they witnessed to him about his need for Jesus Christ. One Friday night, when he had been particularly troubled about what they were saying, he suddenly found himself weeping. Afterward he made a "commitment" to Jesus. They were pleased for him, of course. So was he—until he began to ask what it was that had happened. He had had an experience of some sort. There was no denying that. But he began to wonder whether it was any different from being moved by a good movie. As he spoke about it afterward he said, "I am not even sure that it is as lasting as falling in love, and that does not always last very long. Has anything happened? Am I really saved?"

A student with a Christian background. A student with a non-Christian upbringing. Yet each had missed the same thing. They did not understand that Christianity is neither a set of intellectual beliefs alone, however complete, nor an experience of being "saved," however intense. Rather it is the work of God himself by which one is brought to a knowledge of sin and the need of a Savior, is drawn to that Savior through faith, and is then preserved by him and enabled to grow in him by prayer, Bible study, service and witnessing.

I must say, however, in defense of my two friends—both of whom I gradually became convinced really were Christians—that the confusion they were experiencing was not entirely their fault. Each had been adversely affected by an overemphasis upon one aspect of genuine Christianity to the exclusion of another.

On the one hand, Christians are often overly subjective. They emphasize feeling and experience, detaching these from the work of God in history and the clear propositions of the Word of God. When these are absent or at a low ebb, Christians may try to work up so-called spiritual feelings and fall prey to autosuggestion, circumstances or even the machinations of the devil who, we are told, at times appears to us as "an angel of light" (2 Cor. 11:14).

This overemphasis is not always so extreme, however.

Sometimes it is merely the assumption, often not entirely thought through, that a certain intensity of religious experience is necessary if one is to be saved. Certain kinds of revival meetings suggest this. Or, on a more sophisticated level, one might gain that impression from a book such as *The Varieties of Religious Experience* by William James.[1] This classic study of the psychology of religion attempts to reflect a wide breadth of experience and provide an impartial analysis. People may read this or another book like it and sense, perhaps wrongly, that they are not Christians simply because nothing of comparable intensity has occurred in their lives.

The other danger is equally bad: an overly objective Christian faith. Someone may have vast amounts of biblical knowledge and even a certain intellectual assent and commitment to these truths, but still fail to be changed. There is faith. But it may be the kind of faith James speaks of when he says, "You believe that God is one; you do well. Even the demons believe —and shudder" (Jas. 2:19).

This danger is particularly present among conservative Christians. Harold O. J. Brown says, "Insisting as we rightly do upon the objective nature of the atonement and the effective nature of its application to individual human beings in salvation, we sometimes appear in danger of having a doctrine that is purely historical and judicial, without any believable, human dimensions in the time and space in which we live. . . . [We forget that] we are also in process, and sanctification, the continuing work of the Holy Spirit in our lives, is process" and must exist among us.[2]

How may we avoid these dangers? How shall we solve the problem of having both an objective revelation of God in history and a vital appropriation of that salvation? Left to ourselves there probably is no answer. But the Bible tells us that God has a solution. Just as the Father sent his Son to perform the objective, historical work of the atonement as the ground of our salvation, so also he sends the Holy Spirit to apply that manifold salvation to us personally. This is not one simple and indivisible act. Rather, it involves a series of acts and processes: God's calling, regeneration, justification, adoption, sanctification and glorification. In each case the Holy Spirit applies the work of Christ to us personally.

This book deals with these processes and thus with the work of God's Holy Spirit. As Calvin puts it in the title to the third major section of his *Institutes of the Christian Religion,* it means "the way in which we receive the grace of Christ, what benefits come to us from it, and what effects follow."[3]

Person or Power?
The place to begin in such a discussion is with the nature of the Holy Spirit himself. And the first question is, Should we even use the pronoun *himself?* Is the Holy Spirit a real person whose work it is to save and sanctify us or is he a power which we are to use for our own benefit? If we think of the Holy Spirit as a mysterious power, our thoughts will be, "How can I get more of the Holy Spirit?" If we think of the Holy Spirit as a person, we will ask, "How can the Holy Spirit have more of me?" The first thought is nonbiblical, pagan. The second is New Testament Christianity.

Reuben A. Torrey states clearly,

The conception of the Holy Spirit as a divine influence or power that we are somehow to get hold of and use, leads to self-exaltation and self-sufficiency. One who so thinks of the Holy Spirit and who at the same time imagines that he has received the Holy Spirit will almost inevitably be full of spiritual pride and strut about as if he belonged to some superior order of Christians. One frequently hears such persons say, "I am a Holy Ghost man," or "I am a Holy Ghost woman." But if we once grasp the thought that the Holy Spirit is a divine person of infinite majesty and glory and holiness and power, who in marvellous condescension has come into our hearts to make his abode there and take possession of our lives and make use of

_them, it will put us in the dust and keep us in the dust. I can think of
no thought more humbling or more overwhelming than the thought
that a person of divine majesty and glory dwells in my heart and is
ready to use even me._ [4]

This distinction in outlook is illustrated in the pages of the
New Testament. On the one hand, there is the case of Simon
the magician whose story is told in Acts 8:9-24. Simon was a
citizen of Samaria to which Philip, one of the first deacons,
had come preaching the gospel. Apparently Simon believed
in Christ and was saved, for the account tells us, "Even Simon
himself believed, and after being baptized he continued with
Philip" (v. 13). Simon knew very little about Christianity, however. So when he saw the miracles that were performed and
was amazed by them, he fell into the error of thinking that the
Holy Spirit was a power that could be purchased. Later, when
Peter and John had come to inspect the work in Samaria and
had been used by God to impart the Spirit to others, Simon
offered the disciples money so that they would give him "this
power" (v. 19). Peter replied, "Your silver perish with you, because you thought you could obtain the gift of God with
money! You have neither part nor lot in this matter, for your
heart is not right before God. Repent therefore of this wickedness of yours, and pray to the Lord that, if possible, the intent
of your heart may be forgiven you" (vv. 20-22).

The contrasting example comes from the beginning of the
missionary work involving Paul and Barnabas. In this case we
are told, "While they were worshiping the Lord and fasting,
the Holy Spirit said, 'Set apart for me Barnabas and Saul for
the work to which I have called them' " (Acts 13:2). In the first
example, an individual wanted to get and use God. In the
second example, God got and used two individuals.

But, some may ask, aren't there passages and even whole
sections of the Bible in which the distinct personality of the
Holy Spirit is not evident? This is the case in the Old Testament which often speaks of the Spirit of God as does the sec-

ond verse of Genesis, "And the Spirit of God was moving over the face of the waters," or in reference to certain individuals of whom it is said that "the Spirit of the Lord [God] took possession of" them (Judg. 6:34; 2 Chron. 24:20). These verses may be said to give intimations of the doctrine of the distinct personality of the Holy Spirit and therefore also of the Trinity. But it must be admitted that in the Old Testament there is very little in the way of a clear presentation of the personal distinctness of the second person of the Trinity and even less of the personal distinctness of the Spirit of God.

It is entirely different when we come to the New Testament. Here the Holy Spirit is shown to be one member of the Trinity, equal in all ways to both the Father and Son and yet distinct from them. This does not mean that there are three gods, as indicated in the first volume of this series.[5] There are three persons. But in a way which is beyond our full understanding, these three are also one.

A person is defined as one who has knowledge, feelings and a will, and this is just what is stated of the Spirit. In John 14:16-18 Jesus says regarding the Holy Spirit, "I will pray the Father, and he will give you another Counselor, to be with you for ever, even the Spirit of truth, whom the world cannot receive, because it neither sees him nor knows him; you know him, for he dwells with you, and will be in you." If the Spirit were only a power, this promise would actually be more like compensation: "I am going to be taken from you, but I will give you some*thing* to make up for my departure." But he is not merely a power. He is not a thing which is being given but another divine personality, a personality who has knowledge, for he will know of the disciples' needs; feelings, for he will identify with them in their distress; and will, for he will determine to comfort them in fulfillment of the Lord's commission.

The New Testament evidence for the distinct personality of the Holy Spirit may be grouped in the following six categories:

(1) *The personal actions of the Holy Spirit.* One example is the text just cited. There he is said to comfort Christians. Another is John 16:8-11 which speaks of the Spirit's work of convicting unbelievers. "And when he comes, he will convince the world concerning sin and righteousness and judgment."

(2) *The Holy Spirit's mission distinct from the Father's and the Son's.* Jesus indicates this clearly in his final discourse: "But when the Counselor comes, whom I shall send to you from the Father, even the Spirit of truth, who proceeds from the Father, he will bear witness to me" (Jn. 15:26).

(3) *The Holy Spirit's rank and power, equal to those of the Father and the Son.* The various trinitarian formulas of the New Testament express this clearly. In Matthew 28:19, the disciples are told to baptize "in the name of the Father and of the Son and of the Holy Spirit." In 2 Corinthians 13:14, Paul prays that "the grace of the Lord Jesus Christ and the love of God and the fellowship of the Holy Spirit be with" all his readers. Peter speaks of those who are "chosen and destined by God the Father and sanctified by the Spirit for obedience to Jesus Christ" (1 Pet. 1:2). Jude speaks of our being built up in the Christian faith as we "pray in the Holy Spirit," keep ourselves "in the love of God" and "wait for the mercy of our Lord Jesus Christ unto eternal life" (vv. 20-21).

(4) *The appearances of the Holy Spirit in a visible form.* At the baptism of Jesus, "the Holy Spirit descended upon him in bodily form, as a dove, and a voice came from heaven, 'Thou art my beloved Son; with thee I am well pleased' " (Lk. 3:22). On the day of Pentecost "there appeared to them tongues as of fire, distributed and resting on each one of them" (Acts 2:3).

(5) *The sin against the Holy Spirit.* This implies offense against a personality (Mt. 12:31-32).

(6) *The gifts of the Holy Spirit.* In 1 Corinthians 12:11, after having enumerated the gifts of wisdom, knowledge, faith, healing, miracles, prophecy, the discerning of spirits, tongues

and the interpretation of tongues, Paul writes, "All these are inspired by one and the same Spirit, who apportions to each one individually as he wills."[6] The gifts of the Holy Spirit are distinguished from the Spirit himself, indicating that he is no mere force behind these remarkable displays.

Here are six separate lines of argument showing that the Holy Spirit is a person. Yet the problem for many of us may not be so much with the doctrine of the Holy Spirit as with our attitude toward him. Theoretically many of us do believe that the Holy Spirit is a person, the third person of the Godhead. But do we actually think about him in this way? Do we think about him at all? Perhaps we do what a woman did who had attended a series of messages on the Holy Spirit at a Bible conference years ago. She listened carefully and then came up to the speaker to thank him for his teaching. She said, "Before your messages I never thought of it as a person." Apparently she was not thinking of *him* as a person even yet.

Is He God?

There is one other preliminary matter to be studied. We have insisted that the Holy Spirit is a distinct person, but we have also called him a divine person. Is he divine? Or is he some lesser being, perhaps an angel? Is the Holy Spirit God?

One of the clearest indications of the full divinity of the Holy Spirit is found on the lips of Jesus when he promised to send the Spirit to the disciples to be "another Counselor" (Jn. 14:16). Here the important word is *another*. In Greek there are two different words for *another*. There is *allos,* the word used here (meaning "another just like the first one"), and there is *heteros* (meaning "totally different"), from which we get our word *heterodox*. Since the word *allos* rather than *heteros* occurs in this text, Jesus is saying that he will send the disciples a person just like himself, that is, one who is fully divine. Who is the first Counselor? Jesus. He had been the disciples' strength and counsel during the years of his ministry among them. Now he is going away, and in his place he will be sending a second Counselor who is just like him. He is to be another divine person living with them and (in this case) in them.

This is not the only evidence for this important doctrine, of course. We may gather the evidence for the divinity of the Holy Spirit in the following categories:

(1.) _The divine qualities of the Holy Spirit._ The phrase _Holy Spirit_ is itself a striking example, for the word _holy_ designates the innermost essence of God's nature. He is the "Holy Father" (Jn. 17:11), and Jesus is the "Holy One of God" (Jn. 6:69; compare Mk. 1:24). The Spirit of God is also said to be omniscient (1 Cor. 2:10-11; Jn. 16:12-13), omnipotent (Lk. 1:35) and omnipresent (Ps. 139:7-10).

(2.) _The works of God attributed to the Holy Spirit._ The Spirit was active in the work of creation (see Job 33:4). He imparted the Scriptures (see 2 Pet. 1:21). He is the agent of the new birth, as we will see more fully in a later chapter (see Jn. 3:6). He is the agent of resurrection (see Rom. 8:11).

(3.) _The equality of the Holy Spirit with God the Father and God the Son._ The benedictions and trinitarian formulas cited earlier are examples of this.

(4.) _The name of God indirectly given to him._ The clearest example is in Acts 5:3-4 where Peter says to Ananias, "Ananias, why has Satan filled your heart to lie to the Holy Spirit and to keep back part of the proceeds of the land? . . . You have not lied to men but to God." Other examples are those passages from the Old Testament quoted in the New in which, on the one hand, God is said to be the speaker and in which, on the other hand, the Holy Spirit is said to be speaking. Isaiah 6:8-10 begins, "And I heard the voice of the Lord saying, 'Whom shall I send, and who will go for us?' . . . ." In Acts 28:25-27 the Isaiah passage is quoted, beginning, "The Holy Spirit was right in saying to your fathers through Isaiah the prophet. . . ."

Earlier I attempted to show how it matters practically that

we know that the Holy Spirit is a person. I now ask, Does it
matter that we know that he is God? Yes, it does. If we know
and constantly recognize his deity, we will recognize and rely
on his work. If not, we will inevitably and foolishly rely on our
own limited abilities and forfeit the benefits which he alone
provides. J. I. Packer asks,

> *Do we honor the Holy Spirit by recognizing and relying on his
> work? Or do we slight him by ignoring it, and thereby dishonor,
> not merely the Spirit, but the Lord who sent him? In our faith: do we
> acknowledge the authority of the Bible, the prophetic Old Testa-
> ment and the apostolic New Testament which he inspired? Do we
> read and hear it with the reverence and receptiveness that are due to
> the Word of God? If not, we dishonor the Holy Spirit. In our life:
> do we apply the authority of the Bible, and live by the Bible, what-
> ever men may say against it, recognizing that God's Word cannot
> but be true, and that what God has said he certainly means, and
> will stand to? If not, we dishonor the Holy Spirit, who gave us the
> Bible. In our witness: do we remember that the Holy Spirit alone,
> by his witness, can authenticate our witness, and look to him to do so,
> and trust him to do so, and show the reality of our trust, as Paul did,
> by eschewing the gimmicks of human cleverness? If not, we dishonor
> the Holy Spirit. Can we doubt that the present barrenness of the
> Church's life is God's judgment on us for the way in which we have
> dishonored the Holy Spirit? And in that case, what hope have we of
> its removal till we learn in our thinking and our praying and our
> practice to honor the Holy Spirit? "He shall testify. . . ."*[7]

The personality and deity of the Holy Spirit are practical
teachings, for it is by the activity of this divine being that the
gospel of salvation in Jesus Christ is made clear to us and
changes our lives. He is the key to a vital and truly personal
religion.

2 THE WORK OF THE HOLY SPIRIT

When we are first getting to know a person, in most cases we ask, "Who are you?" and, "What do you do?" The person who answers might say, "I'm Diana Black; I work for the school board" or "I'm Leon Hall; I'm a sales representative with the airline." In each case the first part of the reply contains a name, perhaps coupled with the area from which the individual comes. The second part is about his or her occupation. We can ask the same questions in studying the Holy Spirit. In the last chapter we asked, "Who are you?" We saw that the Holy Spirit is a personal, divine being, equal to God the Father and God the Son in all respects. In this chapter we need to ask what this divine being does.

"He Will Glorify Me"

In asking what the Holy Spirit does we sense almost instinctively that our question is nearly unanswerable. For if the Holy Spirit is God, as he is, then all that the Father and Son do, the Holy Spirit also does. Thus, as I suggested in dealing with the doctrine of the Trinity in volume one of this series, *The Sovereign God,* it is proper to say that the Holy Spirit was active in the creation of the universe (Gen. 1:2), inspired the written Scriptures (2 Pet. 1:21), governed the earthly ministry of the Lord Jesus Christ (Lk. 4:18), gives spiritual life to God's people (Jn. 3:6), and calls forth and directs the church (Acts 13:2; 16:6-7; 20:28). All that the other members of the Godhead do, the Holy Spirit does. On the other hand, we may note that the Bible gives certain emphases to the work of the various members of the Trinity. For example, the Father is principally active in the work of creation and the Son is principally active in the redemption of the human race.

What is the Holy Spirit's primary work? Some would answer by saying that the Holy Spirit is active most in the sanctification of individual believers or in the inspiration of the Bible or in the giving of specific gifts to those serving within the church or in moving unbelievers to accept Christ. But while these items are each examples of things the Spirit does, they are not the best answer to the question. The best answer is found in John 16:13-14 (and related verses) in which Christ himself says of the Spirit's work, "When the Spirit of truth comes, he will guide you into all the truth; for he will not speak on his own authority, but whatever he hears he will speak, and he will declare to you the things that are to come. *He will glorify me,* for he will take what is mine and declare it to you" (my emphasis). In John 15:26, the Lord declares, "He will bear witness to me."

The work of the Holy Spirit is primarily to glorify Christ. Indeed, when they are correctly understood, all the other works that might be mentioned are included within this one overriding purpose.

If we are told that the Holy Spirit will not speak of himself but of Jesus, then we may conclude that any emphasis upon the person and work of the Spirit that detracts from the person and work of Jesus Christ is not the Spirit's doing. In fact, it is the work of another spirit, the spirit of antichrist, whose work it is to minimize Christ's person (1 Jn. 4:2-3). Important as the Holy Spirit is, he is never to pre-empt the place of Christ in our thinking. On the other hand, wherever the Lord Jesus Christ is exalted—in whatever way—there the third person of the Trinity is at work. We may recognize his presence and be thankful for it.

God's Truth

We can now ask, How specifically does the Holy Spirit glorify the Lord Jesus Christ? He does so in four areas.

First, the Holy Spirit glorifies Jesus by teaching about him in the Scriptures. The New Testament tells us that the Holy Spirit was doing this before Christ's Incarnation through the inspiration of the Old Testament. But the work did not stop there. The New Testament records what Christ did and explains its meaning. This was to have such bearing on the work of the disciples that it is emphasized in Christ's final conversations with them. He says, "When the Counselor comes, . . . he will bear witness to me" (Jn. 15:26). And "I have yet many things to say to you, but you cannot bear them now. When the Spirit of truth comes, he will guide you into all the truth" (Jn. 16:12-13).

The disciples knew, no doubt, that in the Old Testament period the Holy Spirit had come upon certain prophets, kings and other leaders in order to speak through them. They might even have understood that the central message of the Old Testament was the promise of God to send a Redeemer. But now they are told that the same Holy Spirit is going to come upon them—indeed, be in them—so that nothing about Christ's work or teachings necessary for our salvation and for the growth of the church might be lost.

How could these people, for the most part unlearned fishermen, be the agents through whom we should receive the New Testament? How can their record of the life and teachings of Jesus be trusted? Perhaps they recorded it incorrectly. Perhaps they mixed truth with error. The answer to these speculations is that they did not make errors because the Holy Spirit guided them and kept them from making mistakes. Some of the events and teachings they recorded were things they had heard and seen and which were brought to their remembrance. Other points were revealed to them later for the first time. In both cases they were led by the Holy Spirit. In fact, it was as true of them as of the Old Testament authors. As Peter said, "No prophecy ever came by the impulse of man, but men moved by the Holy Spirit spoke from God" (2 Pet. 1:21).

In this work the Holy Spirit amply glorified Jesus. The Spirit prepared for Christ's coming through the inspiration of the Old Testament (the Old Testament told people what to expect and when to expect it). Then he preserved the story of his coming and gave the only infallible interpretation of it through the inspiration of the New Testament books.

These verses not only tell us that a new revelation is coming; they also suggest the three-fold nature of this revelation. First, the revelation is *historical.* In John 16:13 Jesus says the Holy Spirit "will guide you [the disciples] into all the truth." That is, he will guide them into the truth concerning Jesus. In John 14:26 the historical element is made even clearer: "He will teach you all things, and bring to your remembrance all that I have said to you." The disciples were likely to forget certain things that happened, but the Holy Spirit would bring to their minds the historical events connected with the life, death and resurrection of Jesus Christ. We have the record of this in the Gospels—Matthew, Mark, Luke, John—and also the book of Acts.

The historical nature of Christianity sets it off dramatically from all other religions, mythologies or philosophies. These conceive of religion largely as a pattern of ideas and of salvation as learning certain things or perhaps doing certain things. Christianity has ideas, that is true; but the ideas are based on what God has actually done, and that is determinative.

This historical basis also cuts Christianity off from the evolutionary view of religion, the view that thousands of years ago men and women had primitive ideas of God which grew as their knowledge grew, and that their writings about God showed this development. Since this has continued to the present, today we can drop what we consider to be unworthy concepts of God and add others we believe to be more valuable. Jesus, on the other hand, taught that far from being disposable, God's own action in history is the very basis of his revelation to men and women. This is seen most clearly in the cross of Christ where God did not just teach an idea, he did something. He atoned for sin, revealed his love and showed judgment. Any understanding of the faith that departs from that historical base is simply not Christianity.

Second, God's revelation is *doctrinal.* Jesus taught that the Holy Spirit "will take what is mine and declare it to you [the disciples]" (Jn. 16:14). "He will teach you all things" (Jn. 14: 26). We have the results of this in the Epistles, beginning with the great letter to the Romans which unfolds Christian doctrine in its fullest form. The other Epistles deal with particular problems in the church and theology, and conclude with those that are pastoral in nature—1 and 2 Timothy, Titus, 1, 2 and 3 John, 1 and 2 Peter, and Jude.

While God has acted in history, we are not left with that alone. He tells us what the action means. Thus, God came in Christ, but the significance of that is that God is revealed to us. We know that God is love because of Christ. We know he is just because of Christ. We know he is compassionately merciful and so much more because of Christ. Again, we say that Christ died. But everyone dies. Why he died is the issue. The Epistles give us the full implications of why Jesus Christ died.

Finally, God's revelation is *prophetic.* Jesus tells us that the

Holy Spirit "will declare to you [the disciples] the things that are to come" (Jn. 16:13). We have the results of this scattered throughout the New Testament: Matthew 24—25; Mark 13; Romans 11; 1 Corinthians 15; and particularly the book of Revelation. Prophecy indicates that God is still at work in history. God does not work in some static way so that our period of history is absolutely identical to earlier periods and to those to come. Rather, God is doing unique things in history—working with people, unfolding a plan—so that what each of us does is important. Moreover, these workings are leading to the day of the Lord's return, at which time God will gather his own out of the world and demonstrate to all that the Lord's way is the only true way. The Holy Spirit has given us the Bible so that in history, in doctrine and in prophecy the Lord Jesus Christ might be glorified.

Born of God

The second way the Holy Spirit glorifies Jesus is by drawing men and women to him in saving faith. I discuss this in detail in part two of this volume, "How God Saves Sinners," so it does not need to be fully expounded now. But I should point out that apart from this activity of the Holy Spirit no one would ever come to Jesus.

After Jesus said that he would send the Holy Spirit to the disciples to be with them forever, he added, "even the Spirit of truth, whom the world cannot receive, because it neither sees him nor knows him" (Jn. 14:17). By *the world* John means the world of men and women who are separate from Christ. Apart from the work of the Holy Spirit in leading people to Christ, no one can either see, know or receive spiritual things. They cannot *see* because they are spiritually blind. As Jesus said, "Unless one is born anew, he cannot see the kingdom of God" (Jn. 3:3). They cannot *know* because the things of the Spirit "are spiritually discerned" (1 Cor. 2:14). They cannot *receive* the Holy Spirit or Christ because, as Jesus said, "No one can come to me unless the Father who sent me draws him" (Jn. 6:44).

So what happens? The Holy Spirit opens blind eyes so that the unregenerate may see the truth, unfogs their minds so that they may understand what they see, and then gently woos their wills until they come to place their faith in the Savior. Without this work there would not be even a single Christian in the world. By means of it the Holy Spirit saves us and glorifies the Lord Jesus.

Reproducing Christ

Third, the Holy Spirit glorifies Jesus by reproducing his character in believers. He does this in three ways: first, by leading Christians to greater victory over themselves and over sin; second, by interceding for them in prayer and by teaching them to pray; and third, by revealing God's will for their lives and by enabling them to walk in it. These ministries combine to produce the "fruit of the Spirit," which is the life of Christ within us.

Paul speaks of this fruit in Galatians 5:22-23, saying, "But the fruit of the Spirit is love, joy, peace, patience, kindness, goodness, faithfulness, gentleness, self-control." These virtues were clearly in Christ to the highest degree and are also to be in all Christians, according to Paul's teaching. Commentators have noted the importance of the fruit being one fruit (singular) instead of fruits (plural). The "fruit of the Spirit" in its entirety is to be present in all. This is not true of the "gifts" of the Spirit, which I will discuss in detail in the fourth and final volume of this series. We are told that the Holy Spirit gives the gifts to one Christian or another as he wills (1 Cor. 12:11). Thus, one may be a teacher, another a pastor, still another an evangelist and so on. By contrast, each and every Christian is to possess all the Spirit's fruit.

Love leads the list, and this is entirely appropriate. "God is love" (1 Jn. 4:8) and, therefore, the greatest of all Christian virtues is love (1 Cor. 13:13). Divine love gives this virtue its character; for God's love is unmerited (Rom. 5:8), great (Eph. 2:4), transforming (Rom. 5:3-5) and unchangeable (Rom. 8:35-39). God's love sent Christ to die for our sin. Now, because the Spirit of Christ is implanted within Christians, we are to show great, transforming, sacrificial and unmerited love both to other Christians and to the world. It is by this that the world is to know that Christians are indeed Christ's followers (Jn. 13:35).

Joy is the virtue that corresponds in the Christian life to happiness in the world. On the surface they seem related. But happiness is dependent on circumstances—when fortunate circumstances are removed, happiness is removed with them —while joy is not. Joy is based on the knowledge of who God is and what he has done for us in Christ. When Jesus was speaking to his disciples about joy just before his arrest and crucifixion, he said, "These things I have spoken to you, that my joy may be in you, and that your joy may be full" (Jn. 15:11). "These things" involve the teachings of John 14—15 and perhaps of John 16 as well since Jesus repeats this saying about joy later (Jn. 17:13). Because of our knowledge of God's acts on our behalf, Christians can be joyful even in the midst of physical suffering, imprisonment or other calamities.

Peace is God's gift to the human race, achieved by him at the cross of Christ. Before the cross we were at war with God. Now God has made peace with us; we are to show the effects of that peace in all circumstances through what we would call "peace of mind" (compare Phil. 4:6-7). Peace is to reign in the home (1 Cor. 7:12-16), between Jews and Gentiles (Eph. 2:14-17), within the church (Eph. 4:3; Col. 3:15) and in the relationships of the believer with everyone else (Heb. 12:14).

Patience is putting up with others even when severely tried. God is the supreme example of patience in his dealings with rebellious people. This fact is held out to us as a reason why we should turn to him from our sin (Joel 2:13; 2 Pet. 3:9).

Kindness is the attitude God has when he interacts with people. God has a right to insist on our immediate and total conformity to his will, and he could be quite harsh with us in getting us to conform. But he is not harsh. He treats us as a good father might treat a learning child (Hos. 11:1-4). This is our pattern. If Christians are to show kindness, they must act toward others as God has acted toward them (Gal. 6:1-2).

Goodness is similar to kindness, but it is most often reserved for situations in which the recipient merits nothing. It is linked to generosity.

Faithfulness means trustworthiness or reliability. Truth, a part of the very character of God, is at issue here. Faithful servants of Christ will die rather than renounce him or, to put it on a less exalted plane, will suffer great inconvenience rather than go back on their word. Those who are faithful do what they say they will do. They will not quit. This is also descriptive of the character of Christ, the faithful witness (Rev. 1:5), and of God the Father who always acts this way toward his people (1 Cor. 1:9; 10:13; 1 Thess. 5:24; 2 Thess. 3:3).

Gentleness or *meekness* (KJV) is seen most clearly in those who are so much in control of themselves that they are always angry at the right time (as against sin) and never angry at the wrong time. It was the pre-eminent virtue of Moses, who is praised for being the gentlest or meekest man then living (Num. 12:3).

The final manifestation of the Spirit's fruit is *self-control* which gives victory over fleshly desires and which is therefore closely related to chastity both of mind and conduct. Barclay notes that it "is that great quality which comes to a man when Christ is in his heart, that quality which makes him able to live and to walk in the world, and yet to keep his garments unspotted from the world."[1]

We must not think, however, that just because these nine virtues are aspects of the Spirit's work and because the Spirit is at work in believers that, therefore, every Christian will automatically possess them. It is not automatic. That is why we are urged to "walk by the Spirit" rather than according to "the flesh" (Gal. 5:16). What makes the difference between a fruitful Christian and a nonfruitful one is closeness to Christ and conscious dependence on him. Jesus taught this in the illustration of the vine and branches: "I am the true vine, and my Father is the vinedresser. Every branch of mine that bears no fruit, he takes away, and every branch that does bear fruit he prunes, that it may bear more fruit. . . . Abide in me, and I in you. As the branch cannot bear fruit by itself, unless it abides in the vine, neither can you, unless you abide in me. I am the vine, you are the branches. He who abides in me, and I in him, he it is that bears much fruit, for apart from me you can do nothing" (Jn. 15:1-2, 4-5).

To be fruitful, the branch which bears the fruit must be attached to the vine. It must be alive and not merely a dead piece of wood. In spiritual terms this means that the individual must first be a Christian. Without the life of Christ within, only the works of the flesh are possible: "fornication, impurity, licentiousness, idolatry, sorcery, enmity, strife, jealousy, anger, selfishness, dissension, party spirit, envy, drunkenness, carousing, and the like" (Gal. 5:19-21). The fruit of the Spirit becomes possible when the life of Christ, conveyed by the Spirit of Christ, flows through the Christian.

There must also be cultivation. This is the point of the opening verse of John 15 in which God is called "the vinedresser." This means that God cares for us, exposing us to the sunshine of his presence, enriching the soil in which we are planted and seeing to it that we are protected from spiritual drought. If we would be fruitful, we must stay close to God through prayer, feed on his Word and keep close company with other Christians.

Finally, there must be pruning. This can be unpleasant at times, for it means that things we treasure will be removed from our lives. Sometimes it may involve suffering. There is a purpose in the pruning, however, and that makes all the difference. The purpose is to bring forth more fruit.

In the Master's Service

The fourth way in which the Holy Spirit glorifies Jesus is by directing Christ's followers into Christian service and by sustaining them in it. This was to be true of the disciples, as most of the verses about the Holy Spirit in the previous pages indicate; he was to direct them in the future in precisely the way Jesus had directed them in the past. This is also true for today's followers of our Lord.

One example is in the passage mentioned for another reason in the last chapter—Acts 13:2-4. "While they were worshiping the Lord and fasting, the Holy Spirit said, 'Set apart for me Barnabas and Saul for the work to which I have called them.' Then after fasting and praying they laid their hands on them and sent them off. So, being sent out by the Holy Spirit, they went down to Seleucia; and from there they sailed to Cyprus." The Holy Spirit calls men and women into specific lines of work and goes with them as they do it.

Of course, he does not always call in precisely the same way. That is probably why we are not told how the disciples at Antioch came to know that the Holy Spirit had designated Barnabas and Saul for missionary work. Again, the fact that he calls does not mean that we should not consciously look for the Holy Spirit's leading. As those in Antioch worshiped the Lord and fasted—that is, as they were taking the work of the Lord seriously and were engaged in it to the best of their ability and knowledge—the Holy Spirit spoke. The same is true for us.

But I am running ahead of myself. Before looking at the Christian life, let us consider how one can become a Christian in the first place. And before that, we should consider the major but difficult biblical doctrine of the union of the Christian with Christ through the Spirit's activity.

3 UNION WITH CHRIST

Marriage is the only union comparable to the union of a Christian with Christ through the work of the Holy Spirit. In both cases all previous loyalties and commitments are superseded by this new covenant. In a mysterious way two distinct individuals join and become one. Let us see if we can gain a better understanding of this mystery.

Past, Present and Future
As with most New Testament teachings, the seeds of this doctrine are in the recorded words of Jesus, in this case conveyed under various metaphors and pictures. One key metaphor is that of the vine and its branches: "Abide in me, and I in you. As the branch cannot bear fruit by itself, unless it abides in the vine, neither can you, unless you abide in me. I am the vine, you are the branches. He who abides in me, and I in him, he it is that bears much fruit, for apart from me you can do nothing" (Jn. 15:4-5). Another metaphor is contained in those expressions which refer to eating Christ as one would eat bread

(Jn. 6:35) or drinking him as one would drink water (Jn. 4: 10-14; compare Mt. 26:26-28). How Christ's followers will be received or rejected by the world suggests the same idea, for this is tantamount to a reception or rejection of himself: "He who hears you hears me, and he who rejects you rejects me, and he who rejects me rejects him who sent me" (Lk. 10:16).

In the high priestly prayer of the Lord recorded in John 17 this union is discussed explicitly: "I do not pray for these only, but also for those who believe in me through their word, that they may all be one; even as thou, Father, art in me, and I in thee, that they also may be in us, so that the world may believe that thou hast sent me. . . . I in them and thou in me, that they may become perfectly one, so that the world may know that thou hast sent me and hast loved them even as thou hast loved me" (vv. 20-21, 23).

In the writings of Paul this doctrine receives its greatest development and emphasis. We think of the important Pauline formulas, "in him," "in Christ," "in Christ Jesus," which occur 164 times in his writings. By use of these phrases, Paul teaches that we are *chosen* "in him before the foundation of the world" (Eph. 1:4), *called* (1 Cor. 7:22), *made alive* (Eph. 2:5), *justified* (Gal. 2:17), *created* "for good works" (Eph. 2:10), *sanctified* (1 Cor. 1:2), *enriched* "with all speech and all knowledge" (1 Cor. 1:5), and *assured of the resurrection* (Rom. 6:5). The apostle says that in Christ alone we have *redemption* (Rom. 3:24), *eternal life* (Rom. 6:23), *righteousness* (1 Cor. 1:30), *wisdom* (1 Cor. 4:10), *freedom* from the law (Gal. 2:4), and every *spiritual blessing* (Eph. 1:3). He gives testimony to his own experience by saying, "I have been crucified with Christ; it is no longer I who live, but Christ who lives in me; and the life I now live in the flesh I live by faith in the Son of God, who loved me and gave himself for me" (Gal. 2:20).

We can tell from these many expressions that the believer's union with Christ is an extremely broad concept, dealing not only with our present experience of Jesus but also reaching back into the eternal past and extending forward into the limitless future.

First, looking back, the fountain of salvation lies in the eternal election of the individual by God the Father in Christ. This is the meaning of the full text from Ephesians 1, parts of which were cited above: "Blessed be the God and Father of our Lord Jesus Christ, who has blessed us in Christ with every spiritual blessing in the heavenly places, even as he chose us in him before the foundation of the world" (Eph. 1:3-4). We may not understand the full meaning of this eternal election in Christ, but at least we can understand that as far back as we can go we find that God's purposes for us involved our salvation. Salvation is not an afterthought. It was there from the beginning.

One commentator has written, "The first work performed by the Holy Spirit in our behalf was to elect us members of Christ's body. In his eternal decrees God determined that he should not be solitary forever, that out of the multitude of sons of Adam a vast host would become sons of God, partakers of the divine nature and conformed to the image of the Lord Jesus Christ. This company, the fulness of him who fills all in all, would become sons by the new birth, but members of the body by the baptism of the Holy Spirit."[1]

Second, in the present we are united with Christ in our regeneration or new birth. Jesus spoke of this to Nicodemus saying, "Unless one is born of water and the Spirit, he cannot enter the kingdom of God" (Jn. 3:5). Paul amplified it noting, "If any one is in Christ, he is a new creation" (2 Cor. 5:17).

We have a picture of our new birth in the physical birth of Jesus Christ. In his birth the sinless and divine life of God the Son was placed within the sinful and quite human body of the virgin Mary. For a time it appeared as if the divine life had been swallowed up. But it eventually revealed itself through the birth of the infant Jesus.

In an analogous way we experience the implantation of the

divine life within us as the Spirit of Christ comes to reside within our hearts. We may say, as did Mary, "But how can this be, seeing that I have no power to beget the divine life myself?" But the answer is in the words of the angel, "The Holy Spirit will come upon you, and the power of the Most High will overshadow you; therefore the child to be born will be called holy, the Son of God" (Lk. 1:35). We do not become divine, as some of the oriental religions believe. But in some sense the very life of God comes to live within us so that we are rightly called sons and daughters of God.

Third, because we were united to Christ in the moment of his death on the cross, redemption from sin has been secured for us, and we are justified from all sin. Paul writes, "Do you not know that all of us who have been baptized into Christ Jesus were baptized into his death?" (Rom. 6:3). And again, "In him we have redemption through his blood" (Eph. 1:7). When Jesus died on the cross those of us who are united to him by saving faith also died with him so far as the punishment of our sin is concerned. God the Father put God the Son to death. Since we are united to him, there is a sense in which we have been put to death too. In this, our sin is punished and we need not fear that it will ever rise up to haunt us. As Henry G. Spafford expressed it in his well-known hymn,

My sin—oh, the bliss of this glorious thought!—
My sin, not in part, but the whole,
Is nailed to his cross, and I bear it no more;
Praise the Lord, praise the Lord, O my soul!

While we are united in Christ's death, we are also united in his life. Paul develops this in the sixth chapter of Romans.

We were buried therefore with him by baptism into death, so that as Christ was raised from the dead by the glory of the Father, we too might walk in newness of life. For if we have been united with him in a death like his, we shall certainly be united with him in a resurrection like his. We know that our old self was crucified with him so that the sinful body might be destroyed, and we might no longer be enslaved to sin. For he who has died is freed from sin. But if we have died with Christ, we believe that we shall also live with him. For we know that Christ being raised from the dead will never die again; death no longer has dominion over him. The death he died he died to sin, once for all, but the life he lives he lives to God. So you also must consider yourselves dead to sin and alive to God in Christ Jesus. (Rom. 6:4-11)

Through our identification with Christ in his death the power of sin over us is broken and we are set free to obey God and grow in holiness.

Finally, looking forward, our identification with Christ in this spiritual union assures our final resurrection (Rom. 6:5; 1 Cor. 15:22) and glorification (Rom. 8:17). Since we are united to Christ, we must eventually be like him. Since we can never be separated from him, we will always be with him (1 Jn. 3:2).

In one sense "union with Christ" is the whole of salvation. Murray writes, "We thus see that union with Christ has its source in the election of God the Father before the foundation of the world and it has its fruition in the glorification of the sons of God. The perspective of God's people is not narrow; it is broad and it is long. It is not confined to space and time; it has the expanse of eternity. Its orbit has two foci, one the electing love of God the Father in the counsels of eternity, the other glorification with Christ in the manifestation of his glory. The former has no beginning, the latter has no end."[2] Apart from Christ we cannot view our state with anything but dread. United to him all is changed, and dread is turned into indescribable peace and great joy.

The Mystery of Union

At this point some may still be asking, "But how am I united to Christ? In what sense have I actually died with him? It all just seems like theological word games." The questions are certainly understandable in view of the real difficulty of this subject. Yet we should seek understanding, as Anselm suggested in his phrase *Fides quarens intellectum,* "Faith in search of understanding." When we do, we find, as is generally the case, that the Bible has already provided much to assist our inquiry, especially in illustrations.

The first is the one I began this chapter with, the illustration of the union of a husband and a wife in marriage. In Ephesians 5 Paul portrays Christ in the role of the husband and the church in the role of the wife. He concludes, "This mystery is a profound one, and I am saying that it refers to Christ and the church" (Eph. 5:32).

What kind of union exists within a good marriage? Obviously, it is a union of love involving a harmony of minds, souls and wills. On the human level we do not always realize this as we should. Yet this is the ideal; and it points quite naturally to our relationship with Christ in which we are enabled increasingly to obey Christ's great commandment: "You shall love the Lord your God with all your heart, and with all your soul, and with all your mind" (Mt. 22:37, a reference to Deut. 6:5). We do not always succeed on this level either but it is the ideal the Holy Spirit moves us toward.

It is possible, however, to conceive of a union of minds, hearts and souls apart from marriage. What makes marriage unique is the new set of legal and social relationships it creates.

Marriage changes the woman's name. She comes into the church as Maria Tower, let us say. She is married to Jim Schultz and leaves the church as Mrs. Schultz. Maria has been identified with her husband by means of the marriage ceremony. In the same way, the name of the believer is changed from Miss Sinner to Mrs. Christian as she is identified with the Lord Jesus.

Accompanying the change of name there are also legal changes. If Maria owned property before the marriage ceremony, she could have sold it as late as that morning with no signature but her own on the document. After the marriage ceremony she can no longer do that, for the legal affairs of her husband and herself are bound up together. This single fact throws penetrating light on the necessity of our union with Christ as the basis of our salvation. For through our union with him, he, our faithful husband and bridegroom, is able to pay the penalty which we have incurred because of our sin.

Finally, there are psychological and social changes. Maria knows that she is a married woman and no longer single. She expects to make adjustments to her new husband and will certainly regard other men quite differently. She may even find herself in new company with new friends and new life goals. In a similar way, when we are united to Christ our old relationships change and Christ becomes the center of our life and existence.

The second illustration of union with Christ is that of the head and the body. In Ephesians 1:22-23 we read, "And he [that is, God the Father] has put all things under his [that is, Christ's] feet and has made him the head over all things for the church, which is his body, the fulness of him who fills all in all." Again, in Colossians 1:18, Paul writes, "He is the head of the body, the church." The fullest development is in 1 Corinthians 12:12-27, which says in part, "For just as the body is one and has many members, and all the members of the body, though many, are one body, so it is with Christ. For by one Spirit we were all baptized into one body—Jews or Greeks, slaves or free—and all were made to drink of one Spirit. . . . Now you are the body of Christ and individually members of it."

This illustration indicates first that our union with Christ is a union with one another as well. As we see in Paul's first letter to the Corinthians, the Christians there were divided, and Paul was striving to impress them with the need to realize their true unity. Second, the "headship" of Christ stresses his lordship. We are all members of the body, but it is *his* body. He is

the head. The body functions properly only when it responds
as he bids it. Third and most important, the illustration shows
the union of head and body as a living and therefore growing
union. This means that the union is not established by the act
of joining some external organization, even a true church.
Rather it is established only when Christ himself takes up resi-
dence within the individual.

The next illustration, that of the vine and the branches (Jn.
15:1-17), highlights that the union of the believer with Christ
is for a purpose: that we might be fruitful, that we might be
useful to God in this world. Note that this fruitfulness is
achieved by Christ's power and not by anything in us. Indeed,
"apart from [him we] can do nothing" (v. 5). Christ also
prunes us, streamlines us for his work so we will be fruitful in
the ways he desires.

The final illustration of the union of the believer with
Christ is the portrait of a spiritual temple composed of many
blocks but with Christ as the foundation: "built upon the foundation of the apostles and prophets, Christ Jesus himself being the cornerstone, in whom the whole structure is joined
together and grows into a holy temple in the Lord; in whom
you also are built into it for a dwelling place of God in the
Spirit" (Eph. 2:20-22). There are parallels to this in Christ's illustration of the "wise man who built his house upon the rock"
(Mt. 7:24) and Paul's other scattered references to ourselves
as "God's building" (1 Cor. 3:9, 11-15). In each of these cases
the central idea is the same: permanence. Because Jesus is
the foundation and is without change, all that is built upon
him will be permanent also. Those who are Christ's will not
perish but will endure to the end.

The Baptism of the Spirit
How does this come about? We have seen that union with
Christ is a legal change. It is a living relationship. It is the
source of divine power within Christians. It is permanent.

How does it happen that we who have had one legal relationship (condemnation) should enter into another in which we become sons and daughters of God? How does it happen that we who were spiritually dead should be made alive, that we who were powerless and without strength should be made strong, that we who are made of dust should live forever? The answer is by the Holy Spirit. Only as the Spirit of Christ unites us to Christ do these truths become realities in our individual experiences.

This is the meaning of the important biblical phrase "the baptism of the Holy Spirit." In our day this phrase is often used to denote experiences linked to the gift of speaking in tongues, which may or may not be from the Holy Spirit. I will discuss these gifts, including the gift of speaking in tongues, in detail in the fourth and final volume of this series. But this use of the phrase is inaccurate. It is also inaccurate to regard the baptism of the Spirit as a second work of grace, as some have done. Certainly the Christian life should be permeated by many works of grace and many fillings by the Spirit (Gal. 5:16; Eph. 5:18). My point is simply that "the baptism of the Spirit" does not refer to these. Rather it describes how all true believers become identified with Christ as members of his mystical body. To understand this phrase best, we should examine the seven passages in the New Testament in which it occurs.

Five of these passages are prophetic in nature. They look forward to the pouring out of God's Spirit on his people in accordance with the Old Testament prophecies, such as Isaiah 32:15; 44:3; and Joel 2:28. The distinctive feature about them is that they are all related to the ministry of Jesus. Thus, on four occasions John the Baptist is quoted as saying, "I baptize you with water for repentance, but he who is coming after me is mightier than I, whose sandals I am not worthy to carry; he will baptize you with the Holy Spirit and with fire" (Mt. 3: 11; parallels in Mk. 1:7-8; Lk. 3:16; and Jn. 1:33). In the fifth instance Jesus is himself quoted as telling the disciples to wait in Jerusalem for the coming of the Holy Spirit at Pentecost, saying, "John baptized with water, but before many days you shall be baptized with the Holy Spirit" (Acts 1:5). In the original Greek Jesus is called "the Baptist" or "the Baptizer" because he baptizes with the Holy Spirit just as John is called "the Baptist" because he baptizes with water.

The sixth reference to the baptism of the Holy Spirit is historic (Acts 11:16). It refers to the simultaneous gift of the Holy Spirit to the household of Cornelius and of the belief of these people in Jesus as a result of Peter's preaching. The reference is significant because it shows that the Holy Spirit was to be given to Gentiles just as he had previously been given to Jews; in other words, that there were not to be two levels or ranks of Christians within the church.

The seventh reference is the most important of all because it is didactic; that is, it is a teaching passage (rather than just a descriptive one). It therefore gives us the doctrine from which the other passages are to be interpreted. In 1 Corinthians 12:13 Paul writes, "For by one Spirit we were all baptized into one body—Jews or Greeks, slaves or free—and all were made to drink of one Spirit." First, we note how the unity of Christians is emphasized here. The Christians at Corinth had allowed their desire for various spiritual gifts to divide them, but Paul writes that they are actually one. His key argument is that they have all been baptized by one Spirit into the one body of Christ. This is an immediate warning to anyone who would allow an emphasis upon a "baptism of the Holy Spirit" defined as a distinctive work of grace to divide Christians and destroy fellowship.

Second, we see that this experience is universal for all believers. Here the word *all* is decisive, for Paul writes that "we were *all* baptized" and that "*all* were made to drink of one Spirit." In other words, the baptism of the Holy Spirit is not a secondary and special experience for some Christians but rather the initial experience of all by which, indeed, they became Christians in the first place. Baptism signifies identification with Christ. It is the Holy Spirit's role to identify us with Christ and, therefore, with his spiritual body, the church. This he does by engendering faith in our hearts while, at the same time, engrafting us into God's family.

John R. W. Stott, in a valuable study of these verses, summarizes the evidence like this: "The 'gift' or 'baptism' of the Spirit, one of the *distinctive* blessings of the new covenant, is a *universal* blessing for members of the new covenant, because it is an *initial* blessing. It is part and parcel of belonging to the new age. The Lord Jesus, the mediator of the new covenant and the bestower of its blessings, gives both the forgiveness of sins and the gift of the Spirit to all who enter his covenant. Further, baptism with water is the sign and seal of baptism with the Spirit, as much as it is of the forgiveness of sins. Water-baptism is the initiatory Christian rite, because Spirit-baptism is the initiatory Christian experience."[3]

But what of the description of the coming of the Holy Spirit at Pentecost and the accompanying gift of tongues? Doesn't this suggest that speaking in tongues (or some other spectacular gift) should be the normative and desired experience of Christians, whatever the technical meaning of the phrase "baptism of the Spirit" might mean?

We must think it through clearly. First, if the baptism of the Holy Spirit is the "initiatory Christian experience," as Stott says, and if speaking in tongues or some other spectacular gift is the necessary evidence of that baptism, then none who have not had this experience are saved. This is a drastic conclusion, which few would make, since salvation is based solely on faith in the Lord Jesus Christ as Savior, and many who have not had the gift of tongues or some other spectacular gift clearly make such profession. But the conclusion does follow from linking the experience of Pentecost to the baptism. Most who advocate the necessity of the Pentecostal experience avoid this by speaking of a second work of grace, but without biblical warrant.

When we turn to passages that deal explicitly with gifts and baptism, we find that they are quite balanced. The exercise of the gift of tongues is not forbidden (1 Cor. 14:39). It is a valid spiritual gift (1 Cor. 12:4-11). But while every Christian has at least one gift not all have *this* one (1 Cor. 12:29-30), and we are not encouraged to seek it more than others (1 Cor. 14:1-5). The various listings of the gifts in 1 Corinthians might be read as suggesting that tongues—which always comes last—is relatively low in any listing of gifts by importance.

Why then does Luke emphasize the gift of tongues in his account of Pentecost? It would be enough to say that he does so simply because this is what happened in fulfillment of the prophecy in Joel. But if a theological meaning is sought—which we have every right to do since Luke was a theologically oriented historian and no mere chronicler of dates and facts—this is to be found in the ultimate effect of Pentecost: the proclamation of the gospel and a widespread response to it—not merely the tongues experience. Charles E. Hummel has written a book in which one chapter attempts to bridge the unnecessary gaps between Pentecostal and non-Pentecostal theologies. He denies the distinction, which I have made, between descriptive and didactic passages. Even so, when he comes to speak of Luke's unique theological emphasis, he focuses not on the experience of tongues but on the expansion of the gospel. "According to Luke's teaching, the baptism in the Spirit for the disciples was an empowering for prophetic witness."[4]

Actually, at this point Luke's distinctive theology is better expressed by the more commonly used phrase "fullness of [or filled with] the Holy Spirit." There are thirteen of these references, four describing events or circumstances before Pentecost took place (which are therefore more in line with

Old Testament experiences), and nine describing events or circumstances after Pentecost. The first four, all in Luke, refer to Christ (4:1), John the Baptist (1:15), Elizabeth, the mother of John (1:41) and Zachariah, John's father (1:67). The remaining nine are in the book of Acts and are descriptive. (One additional reference in Paul's writings is Eph. 5:18.)

Regarding the nine verses from Acts we notice that the company waiting in the upper room on the day of Pentecost was filled with the Spirit (2:4), that Peter received a special filling before speaking to the Sanhedrin (4:8), that the early Christians were filled with the Spirit on one occasion following prayer, as a result of which they began to speak "the word of God with boldness" (4:31), that the first deacons were chosen on the basis of being men "full of the Spirit" (6:3), that Stephen, the first martyr, being "full . . . of the Holy Spirit" (6:5), saw Jesus standing at the right hand of the Father and testified of this fact (7:55), that Paul was filled with the Spirit when Ananias placed his hands upon him, having been sent to him following his experience on the road to Damascus (9:17), that Paul was "filled with the Holy Spirit" on another occasion as a result of which he confronted Elymas, the sorcerer, on Paphos (13:9), and that Barnabas (11:24) and the disciples at Antioch were also each filled with the Spirit in other instances (13:52).

What is characteristic of these nine descriptions is not any external or supernatural manifestation of the Spirit such as a speaking in tongues, for that is associated only with the one reference to the filling with the Spirit at Pentecost. The only thing that is characteristic of all nine passages is that in every instance the person or group of persons who received the filling immediately began to testify to the Christian gospel. That is, they began to bear witness to Christ. The one hundred twenty did so at Pentecost. Peter did so before the Sanhedrin. So did the early disciples mentioned in Acts 4. Stephen, Paul, Barnabas, and the disciples at Antioch are other examples.

The only apparent exception is the reference to the first deacons. But on closer examination we see that this is not a true exception, for we are not told of a filling of the deacons by the Spirit. We are only told that they were men who gave evidence that their lives had already been filled by the Spirit. How was this known? Perhaps by the fact that they were already active as witnesses. The account of the choice of these deacons is immediately followed by the story of the death of the deacon Stephen, which contains an extensive and effective witness.

To return to the matter of the baptism of the Holy Spirit, we conclude that this is for all Christians and is the equivalent of our being united to Christ in salvation. On the other hand, Christians are also to be filled with the Holy Spirit, an experience of grace which will express itself in witness to Christ. There is not a single instance in the New Testament in which any believer is urged to be baptized with the Holy Spirit or even commanded to be, for the simple reason that he cannot be urged to seek something that has already taken place in his life. But we are to be filled with the Spirit, the source of any successful witness of the church to Jesus Christ.[5]

PART II
HOW GOD SAVES SINNERS

Jesus answered him, "Truly, truly, I say to you, unless one is born anew, he cannot see the kingdom of God." (Jn. 3:3)

For by grace you have been saved through faith; and this is not your own doing, it is the gift of God—not because of works, lest any man should boast. (Eph. 2:8-9)

And to one who does not work but trusts him who justifies the ungodly, his faith is reckoned as righteousness. (Rom. 4:5)

Every one who believes that Jesus is the Christ is a child of God, and every one who loves the parent loves the child. By this we know that we love the children of God, when we love God and obey his commandments. (1 Jn. 5:1-2)

For all who are led by the Spirit of God are sons of God. For you did not receive the spirit of slavery to fall back into fear, but you have received the spirit of sonship. (Rom. 8:14-15)

"I do not pray that thou shouldst take them out of the world, but that thou shouldst keep them from the evil one. They are not of the world, even as I am not of the world. Sanctify them in the truth; thy word is truth." (Jn. 17:15-17)

4 THE NEW BIRTH

The birth of a baby is a wonderful thing. It is wonderful to the mother and father. But it is also wonderful to the doctors and nurses who often continue to speak in awe of the "miracle" of birth even though they have witnessed the entry of hundreds or even thousands of children into this world. On some occasions, as in the birth of a child to well-known parents, the news is reported by the newspapers, radio and television.

None of these human births, however, can compare to the supernatural birth of a child of God through God's Spirit. The world around may take little interest in the occurrence. Few of the world's people took notice of the birth of Christ. Yet the angels celebrated the nativity with their nighttime song in the sky over the fields of Bethlehem. In the same way, few note the birth of a child of God today. Yet as Jesus said, "There is joy before the angels of God over one sinner who repents" (Lk. 15:10).

The birth of a child of God is a spiritual resurrection, the passage of one into new life who formerly was dead in trespasses and sins. A child of wrath becomes a child of the Father who is in heaven. The theological term for this new birth is regeneration.

The Sequence of Salvation

Important as regeneration is, it is not the whole of salvation and should not be seen as an end in itself. John Murray notes in *Redemption Accomplished and Applied* that just as God made the earth teem with good things to satisfy men and women, so he showered us with an abundance of good in our salvation. "This superabundance appears in the eternal counsel of God respecting salvation; it appears in the historic accomplishment of redemption by the work of Christ once for all; and it appears in the application of redemption continuously and progressively till it reaches its consummation in the liberty of the glory of the children of God."[1] The words *continuously* and *progressively* indicate that the new birth, though of maximum importance, is but one step in an eternal process. While the accomplishment of our salvation by the death of Jesus was a single event, its application comprises a series of acts and processes which are called the *ordo salutis* or "steps [of God's] salvation."

What are they? One obvious act is the determining choice of God which comes before the new birth. Verses like John 1: 12-13 point to this. Those who become "children of God" become so "not of blood nor of the will of the flesh nor of the will of man, but of God." Similarly, James 1:18 declares, "Of his own will he brought us forth by the word of truth that we should be a kind of first fruits of his creatures."

Other acts and processes follow the new birth. John 3:3 tells us that "unless one is born anew, he cannot see the kingdom of God," and John 3:5 adds, "unless one is born of water and the Spirit, he cannot enter the kingdom of God." The new birth must come before we see the kingdom of God and enter.

Another helpful statement is 1 John 3:9. "No one born of God commits sin; for God's nature abides in him, and he cannot sin because he is born of God." John is not talking about perfection in this verse, for earlier he has insisted that Christians do sin. If they claim differently, they are either deceived or lying—"If we say we have no sin, we deceive ourselves, and the truth is not in us" (1:8). He is talking about sanctification, which follows regeneration and is the progressive growth in holiness of one who has become God's child.

Romans 8:28-30 adds justification and glorification. "We know that in everything God works for good with those who love him, who are called according to his purpose. For those whom he foreknew he also predestined to be conformed to the image of his Son, in order that he might be the first-born among many brethren. And those whom he predestined he also called; and those whom he called he also justified; and those whom he justified he also glorified." In these verses foreknowledge and predestination deal with the prior determination by God. Calling, justification and glorification deal with the application of redemption directly to us. We know from Paul's teaching elsewhere that justification presupposes faith (Rom. 5:1), so we can insert faith before justification, but after regeneration. Sanctification follows justification and obviously comes before glorification. In the final pattern we have: God's foreknowledge, predestination, then his effectual call of us, regeneration, faith and repentance, justification, sanctification and glorification.[2]

These steps could be subdivided and in some cases perhaps even combined with no great loss. But this is the general sequence presented in Scripture and therefore a most helpful one in coming to see how God actually saves us. Before everything there stands God's eternal election. Where our personal experience is concerned, the first step is our spiritual regeneration.

Divine Initiative

Rebirth is a metaphor of the initial step in salvation. Its use goes back to Jesus himself. He did not mean to teach the need for a literal, physical rebirth. That would be nonsense, as Nicodemus recognized. "How can a man be born when he is old? . . . How can this be?" (Jn. 3:4, 9). Rather Jesus wished to point to the need for a new beginning. We had a beginning once in Adam. It was a good beginning. But we have ruined that through our sin. What we need now is a new start in which "the old has passed away" and "the new has come" (2 Cor. 5:17).

The metaphor of rebirth also points out that regeneration is God's work and not the work of sinful human beings. One cannot be born physically by his or her own doing. It is only as a human egg and sperm join, grow and finally enter this world that birth occurs—a process initiated and nurtured by the parents. Likewise spiritual rebirth is initiated and nurtured by our heavenly parent and is outside our own doing.

The very first reference to the new birth in John's Gospel, John 1:12-13, tells us more. "But to all who received him, who believed in his name, he gave power to become children of God; who were born, not of blood nor of the will of the flesh nor or the will of man, but of God." Each of these three negatives—not of blood nor of the will of the flesh nor of the will of man—is important.

"Not of blood" means that regeneration is not by virtue of *physical birth*. To some people, having a certain bloodline is quite important. In Jesus' day there were thousands of Jews who thought that they were right with God simply because they were descendants of Abraham (Jn. 8:33). They were like Paul, who boasted that he was "circumcised on the eighth day, of the people of Israel, of the tribe of Benjamin, a Hebrew born of Hebrews" (Phil. 3:5). Abraham had received promises from God that he would be with him and his spiritual descendants forever. So the Jews thought they had it made just because they were descended from Abraham physically. Jesus pointed out that God was interested in a spiritual relationship and that their actions indicated that they were actually children of the devil (Jn. 8:44). In the same way, many people today think that they are right with God simply because they have been born of Christian parents or in a so-called Christian country. But physical birth saves no one.

"Nor of the will of the flesh" is more difficult to interpret. St. Augustine, who took the phrase "not of blood" to refer to human birth (as I have also done), took "nor of the will of the flesh" to be the woman's part in reproduction and the phrase "nor of the will of man" to be the man's part. Luther referred to "the will of the flesh" as an act of adoption, Frederick Godet to the sensual imagination, Calvin to will power. Can these differences be resolved? Perhaps, if we consider that in the New Testament the word *flesh* signifies our natural appetites, our sensual or emotional desires. We may therefore come closest to John's meaning by saying that a people cannot become children of God by exercising their *feelings or emotions.*

Some today believe that they are Christians simply because they get an emotional kick out of attending a certain kind of church service or because they were once moved to tears at an evangelistic rally. Emotion may well accompany a genuine experience of the new birth, but the new birth is not produced by that emotion.

The third phrase, "nor of the will of man," is easier to understand. No one can become a child of God by sheer *volition.* In this life we can get ahead through determination, but we cannot be born again this way. You may have little of this world's goods, basic values, education or ability. Nevertheless, you might work doggedly, go to night school, get a better job, and eventually become quite rich. You might enter politics and perhaps rise to be a congressional representative or even president. Others will praise you and call your effort a story of determination combined with a bit of good fortune. But nothing will make you the natural son or daughter of one set of parents if you have been born to another. And nothing will make you a child of God unless God himself brings about a new birth.

Becoming a child of God requires God's grace. While we must believe on Jesus as the divine Savior to become Christians, we believe because God himself has taken the initiative to plant his divine life within us.

Wind and Water

The image of rebirth also helps us understand what happens when God takes the initiative in salvation. Nicodemus came to Christ to talk about spiritual reality, but Jesus replied to Nicodemus's remarks by saying that no one can understand, much less enter into spiritual realities, unless he or she is born again. The word translated "again" is *anothēn* which means not merely "again" but "from above." Jesus was telling Nicodemus that he must first be the recipient of this free grace from God. But Nicodemus did not understand. " 'How can a man be born when he is old? Can he enter a second time into his mother's womb and be born?' Jesus answered, 'Truly, truly, I say to you, unless one is born of water and the Spirit, he cannot enter the kingdom of God. . . . The wind blows where it wills, and you hear the sound of it, but you do not know whence it comes or whither it goes; so it is with every one who is born of the Spirit' " (Jn. 3:4-5, 8). Having identified the source of the new birth, Jesus then spoke of how regeneration occurs.

But what does it mean to be "born of water and the Spirit"? And why does Jesus mention "wind"? There are a number of explanations. The first takes *water* to mean physical birth (in which the appearance of the baby is accompanied by the release of the amniotic fluid from the mother) and *wind (spiritus)* to mean the Holy Spirit. According to this view, Jesus is saying that for a person to be saved he or she must first be born physically and then spiritually.

No one can fault the conclusion itself. Indeed to be saved one must certainly first be physically alive and then also be born again spiritually. But that does not seem to be Christ's meaning. For one thing, the word _water_ is never used in this way elsewhere in Scripture. Our thoughts along those lines are modern. Second, a reference to the necessity of physical birth is so self-evident that one wonders if Jesus would have wasted his words in this fashion. Third, _water_ cannot refer to physical birth because, as we saw in John 1:13, physical birth has no bearing on regeneration.

A second interpretation of this phrase would take _water_ to mean the water of Christian baptism. But baptism is simply not in view in this chapter. Indeed, the Bible teaches that no one can be saved by any external rite of religion (1 Sam. 16: 7; Rom. 2:28-29; Gal. 2:15-16; 5:1-6). Baptism is an important sign of what has already taken place, but it is not the means by which we are regenerated.

The third interpretation takes both _water_ and _wind_ symbolically. Water, so the argument goes, refers to cleansing; wind refers to power. So one must be both cleansed and filled with power.[3] While sinners must be cleansed from their sin and while it is our privilege as Christians to be given power from on high, it is hard to think that this is the meaning of the passage. For one thing, in the rest of the New Testament, cleansing and power accompany the new birth or are said to follow it while these verses deal with the way in which the new birth itself comes about. Moreover, neither cleansing nor power are at all related to the birth metaphor, as seems to be required.

Kenneth S. Wuest has proposed a fourth explanation based on the use of _water_ as a metaphor in other New Testament texts. _Water_ is often used in Scripture to refer to the Holy Spirit. In John 4, for instance, Jesus tells the woman of Samaria that he will give her "a spring of water welling up to eternal life" (Jn. 4:14). The language of John 7:37-38 is almost identical to that of 4:14. John himself adds, "Now this he said about the Spirit, which those who believed in him were to receive" (v. 39). Wuest also refers to Isaiah 44:3 and 55:1, both of which should have been known to Nicodemus. If this is the correct interpretation, "of water and the Spirit" is a repetition of ideas. The word *and* should be taken in its emphatic sense. In English this is generally indicated by using the word *even*. Jesus would be saying, "Truly, truly, I say to you, unless one is born of water, even of the Spirit, he cannot enter God's kingdom."[4]

The explanation given by Wuest is good, but I have always felt that more can be said. Besides being a metaphor for the Spirit, water is also used in the Bible to refer to the Word of God. Ephesians 5:26 says that Christ loved the church and gave himself up for her "that he might sanctify her, having cleansed her by the washing of water with the word." In 1 John 5:8, the same author who composed the fourth Gospel writes of "three witnesses, the Spirit, the water, and the blood." Since he then goes on to speak of God's written witness to the fact that salvation is in Christ, the Spirit must refer to God's witness within the individual, the blood to the historical witness of Christ's death and the water to the Scriptures. The same imagery lies behind John 15:3: "You are already made clean by the word which I have spoken to you." Another important text actually cites the Scriptures as the channel through which the new birth comes about although without using water as a metaphor. James 1:18 reads, "Of his own will he brought us forth by the word of truth that we should be a kind of first fruits of his creatures."

When we consider Christ's words to Nicodemus in the light of these passages, we are able to think of God as the divine begetter, the Father of his spiritual children, and of the Word of God employed by the Holy Spirit as the means by which new spiritual life is engendered. That is, in John 3:5 Jesus is using two images: water and wind. The first stands for the Word of God, the second for the Holy Spirit. He is teaching that as the Word is shared, taught, preached or otherwise made known, the Holy Spirit uses it to bring forth new spiritual life in those whom God is saving. That is why the Bible tells us that it pleased God to save us by the foolishness of preaching (1 Cor. 1:21; Rom. 10:14-15).

Spiritual Conception

One more verse dealing with the new birth makes what I have been saying clearer. 1 Peter 1:23 says, "You have been born anew, not of perishable seed but of imperishable, through the living and abiding word of God."

In this chapter of 1 Peter, the apostle has said that a person enters the family of God because of Christ's death (vv. 18-19) and through faith (v. 21). Peter then goes on to emphasize that God is the Father of his children by likening the Word of God to human sperm. The Latin Vulgate makes this clearer than our English versions, for the word used there is _semen_.

Let's put the teachings and images of these passages together. God first plants within our heart what we might call the ovum of saving faith, for we are told that even faith is not of ourselves, it is the "gift of God" (Eph. 2:8). Second, he sends forth the seed of his Word, which contains the divine life within it, to pierce the ovum of faith. The result is conception. Thus, a new spiritual life comes into being, a life that has its origin in God and no connection to the sinful life that surrounds it.

By our rebirth we are initiated into an entirely new series of relationships and duties within God's family. But no one who has believed on Jesus Christ is to take these doctrines as an excuse for doing as he or she pleases. In part three we will see how we are to live out this new life.[5]

5   FAITH AND REPENTANCE

Rebirth is the first point at which the saving activity of God touches us as individuals. But in God's economy regeneration is inseparable from what follows. Next in the sequence are faith and its accompanying grace, repentance.

Faith is the indispensable channel of salvation. In Hebrews 11:6 we are told that *"without faith* it is impossible to please [God]." Ephesians 2:8-9 declares, "For by grace you have been saved *through faith;* and this is not your own doing, it is the gift of God—not because of works, lest any man should boast." Even John 3:16, which uses the verbal form of the word "faith" ("believe") rather than the noun, says, "For God so loved the world that he gave his only Son, that *whoever believes* in him should not perish but have eternal life." But what is faith?

What Faith Is Not
Let us begin by considering what faith is not. A great deal of

confusion exists about faith simply because we inevitably apply the word to people who are untrustworthy. For example, we speak about doing something in "good faith." But in anything important we do not accept the mere word of the individual. We require deeds, contracts and other written guarantees. In money matters we require collateral. Why? Because, although each side wants to believe in the good faith of the other, each also knows that people cannot always be trusted and must therefore be bound by formal agreements. It is easy to see why faith has often taken on overtones of wishful thinking.

Most commonly, faith is misunderstood as being *subjective*. This is the faith of religious feeling divorced from the objective truth of God's revelation. A number of years ago in a rather extended discussion about religion a young man told me that he was a Christian. As our conversation developed I discovered that he did not believe that Jesus Christ was fully divine. He said that Jesus was God's Son, but only in the sense that we are all God's sons. He did not believe in the resurrection. He did not believe that Jesus died for our sin or that the New Testament contains an accurate record of his life and ministry. He did not acknowledge Christ as Lord of his life. When I pointed out that these beliefs are involved in any true definition of a Christian, he answered that nevertheless he believed deep in his heart that he was a Christian. The thing he called faith turned out to be a certain variable outlook on life grounded in his feelings.

Another common substitute for faith is *credulity*. Credulity is the attitude of people who will accept something as true apart from evidence simply because they earnestly wish it to be true. Rumors of miraculous cures for some incurable disease sometimes encourage this attitude. This is faith of a sort, but it is not what the Bible means by faith.

A third substitute for true faith is *optimism*, a positive mental attitude which is to cause the thing believed in to happen. An example would be sales representatives who so intensely believe in their ability to sell that they actually become successful.

Norman Vincent Peale popularized this outlook in a best-selling book called _The Power of Positive Thinking_. He suggests that we collect a number of the strongest statements about faith in the New Testament, memorize them, allow them to sink down into our subconscious minds and transform us, and thus become believers in God and in ourselves. If we memorize verses like "All things are possible to him who believes" (Mk. 9:23) and "If you have faith as a grain of mustard seed, you will say to this mountain, 'Move from here to there,' and it will move; and nothing will be impossible to you" (Mt. 17:20), we will be able to do what we previously thought impossible. Peale concludes, "According to your faith in yourself, according to your faith in your job, according to your faith in God, this far will you get and no further."[1]

Apparently in Peale's mind faith in oneself, faith in one's job and faith in God are linked together, and what this really means is that the object of faith is irrelevant. John R. W. Stott writes, "He [Peale] recommends as part of his 'worry-breaking formula' that the first thing every morning before we get up we should say out loud 'I believe' three times, but he does not tell us in what we are so confidently and repeatedly to affirm our belief. The last words of his book are simply 'so believe and live successfully.' But believe _what_? Believe _whom_? To Dr. Peale faith is really another word for self-confidence, for a largely ungrounded optimism."[2] Of course, there is some value in a positive mental attitude. It can help you do your work better. But this is not faith in the biblical sense.

Against these distortions we must reply that real faith is not at all based on a person's individual attitudes and feelings. In the context of these human definitions faith is unstable. In the context of biblical teaching faith is reliable, for it is faith in the trustworthy God, who reveals himself reliably.

Faith: The Title Deed

This is why faith can be called "the assurance of things hoped for, the conviction of things not seen" (Heb. 11:1). Some have used this verse as if it were suggesting a "pie-in-the-sky-by-and-by" type of religion. But this sole definition of faith in the entire Bible actually teaches the reverse. The word *assurance* does not mean "substitute for evidence," which is what the word *substance* (used in the King James Bible) suggests to many people. It actually means a "title deed to a piece of property." Although none of us have entered into the fullness of the inheritance that is ours through faith in Christ, faith is our title deed to it. Faith is itself the evidence of things not yet fully seen.

If this were a human title deed, there would still be room for doubt. But in dealing with God doubt is unwarranted because of God's nature. He is the God of truth, so whatever he declares can be trusted. He is infallible, so whatever he declares can be trusted completely. He is faithful. If he promises something, we know that he will stand by that promise. He is omnipotent, all-powerful. Nothing can possibly rise up to frustrate the fulfillment of his desires.

When God calls us to believe in Christ, he is calling us to do the most sensible thing we can ever do. He is asking us to believe the Word of the only being in the universe who is entirely reliable.

This is what John is getting at when he writes, "If we receive the testimony of men, the testimony of God is greater" (1 Jn. 5:9). John is drawing a contrast between the way in which we trust others, even though they are untrustworthy, and the way we ought to trust God. We trust other human beings every day of our lives. When we drive our car across a bridge, we have faith that the bridge will hold us up. We have faith in the engineer who designed it, in the people who built and maintain it and in the inspectors who guarantee its safety —even though we have probably never met any of them. If we

get on a bus to go home from a party some night, we have faith
that the bus is safe, that the driver is an employee of the trans-
portation company, that the sign on the bus is a true indication
of where the bus is going. If we buy a ticket to a sports event,
we have faith that the show will be held as advertised and that
the ticket will gain us admission. John argues that if we can
do this with other human beings who are often untrustworthy, we can do it with God. Indeed, we must. For God commands faith, and the salvation of our souls must express itself
through responses to his offer.

Bringing the Knowledge of Faith

True biblical faith has intellectual content, the point which
Calvin emphasizes in the chapter on faith in his *Institutes of the
Christian Religion*.[3] He stresses that faith's object is Christ, that
faith rests upon knowledge rather than pious ignorance, that
this necessary knowledge comes from God's Word, that faith
involves certainty, that the Bible is its shield and so on. He
declares, "We shall possess a right definition of faith if we call
it a firm and certain knowledge of God's benevolence toward
us, founded upon the truth of the freely given promise in
Christ, both revealed to our minds and sealed upon our hearts
through the Holy Spirit."[4]

This knowledge involves who Jesus is (the second person
of the Godhead, born of the virgin Mary, clothed in our nature, offered up for our transgressions and raised again for
our justification), who we are (sinners who need a Savior) and
much besides. The Holy Spirit is the one who brings this
knowledge of the gospel to us. In John 16 Jesus tells us, "And
when he [the Holy Spirit] comes, he will convince the world
concerning sin and righteousness and judgment: concerning
sin, because they do not believe in me; concerning righteousness, because I go to the Father, and you will see me no more;
concerning judgment, because the ruler of this world is
judged" (vv. 8-11).

The Holy Spirit convicts the world of sin because, as Jesus immediately explains, "They do not believe in me." This may mean, "He will convict the world of wrong ideas of sin which they have because they do not believe," "He will convict the world of its sin because, without this conviction, they do not believe" or "He will convict the world of the sin of unbelief."[5] Any of these translations is possible, and John may even be suggesting more than one, as is his manner. But if conviction with a view to salvation is the major thought of this passage, as it seems to be, then the second interpretation is primary. The primal sin is putting self at the center of life and so spurning belief. Understanding this is essential for salvation.

The third interpretation includes the truth that the Holy Spirit is like a prosecuting attorney who secures a verdict of "guilty" against the world. The second interpretation adds that he brings this guilt home to the human consciousness so that men and women are disturbed by sin and seek freedom from it.

For example, on the day of Pentecost the disciples gathered together to await the coming of the Holy Spirit. When he came, they went into the streets of Jerusalem and Peter preached that the coming of the Holy Spirit was the fulfillment of the prophecy of Joel, given to call men and women to Christ and salvation. Peter then preached Jesus, concluding his sermon by saying, "Let all the house of Israel therefore know assuredly that God has made him both Lord and Christ, this Jesus whom you crucified." We are told that immediately, "when they heard this they were cut to the heart, and said to Peter and the rest of the apostles, 'Brethren, what shall we do?' " (Acts 2:36-37). When Peter answered their question three thousand believed and were baptized.

This was a remarkable response, but it was not due to Peter's brilliant analysis of the gospel or to his eloquence. If he had preached this sermon the day before, nothing would have happened. No one would have believed. He and the others would have been laughed at. But the Holy Spirit on Pentecost came and convicted the people of their sin. This is why they were "cut to the heart" and asked, "What shall we do?" As faith was born in their hearts, repentance followed. They wanted freedom from the sin they suddenly saw in their lives.

Not everyone has believed that we are unable to convict ourselves or others of sin. This lay at the heart of the controversy between Pelagius and Augustine and later between Arminius and the followers of Calvin. Neither Pelagius nor Arminius denied that salvation was by grace. But they did deny that it was _all_ of grace, that we make no move toward God unless God first convicts and then draws us. Pelagius said that our will is always free and that it can therefore always choose or reject anything offered to it. As to the gospel, grace makes the offer. But the ultimate criterion by which we are either saved or lost is our will. Pelagius did not understand that it is impossible for us either to become aware of our sin or to understand and respond to the gospel without the Holy Spirit's activity in our lives.[6]

Second, the Holy Spirit convinces people "concerning righteousness," says Jesus, "because I go to the Father, and you will see me no more." This can mean that the Holy Spirit will show the world what true righteousness is since Jesus is no longer here to demonstrate the meaning of righteousness in his own person. Or Jesus' words could mean that the Holy Spirit will show the world where divine righteousness may be found. It cannot be found here. We cannot save ourselves by any human righteousness. But what is needed is in Christ who was once here but is now at the Father's right hand.

Lastly, the Spirit convicts the world "concerning judgment, because the ruler of this world is judged." The best understanding of these words seems to be that the Holy Spirit will convince the world that there is such a thing as judgment, which is proved by the judgment of Satan and the breaking of his power at the cross.

Nobody wants to believe in judgment. We want to think that we can do what we wish with impunity and that no day of reckoning will come. We are even encouraged in this thought because God does not always judge immediately, and evil often seems to go unpunished. This, of course, is false thinking. God does not always judge sinners immediately because he is long-suffering. Still, the judgments will come eventually. God's judgment on Satan is proof. Peter makes the same point. After showing that God judged the fallen angels, the world of Noah's time, and the cities of Sodom and Gomorrah, he concludes, "The Lord knows how to rescue the godly from trial, and to keep the unrighteous under punishment until the day of judgment" (2 Pet. 2:9).

Love and Commitment
While a rational concept of Christianity is needed for faith, we cannot forget that the devil also understands these things and is probably more orthodox than most. True biblical faith therefore also requires a moving of the heart, much like that described by John Wesley in telling how his heart was "strangely warmed" as a result of the little meeting in Aldersgate.

Calvin was no less concerned to stress the heart as well as the intellect in faith. At one point he says, "It now remains to pour into the heart itself what the mind has absorbed. For the Word of God is not received by faith if it flits about in the top of the brain, but when it takes root in the depth of the heart that it may be an invincible defense to withstand and drive off all the stratagems of temptation.... The Spirit accordingly serves as a seal, to seal up in our hearts those very promises the certainty of which it has previously impressed upon our minds; and takes the place of a guarantee to confirm and establish them."[7] In another place he concludes, "It follows that faith can in no wise be separated from a devout disposition."[8]

Finally, faith is also trust or commitment. We turn from trusting in ourselves and instead trust God fully. We see the infinite worth and love of the Son of God, who gave himself for our salvation, and commit ourselves to him.

Marriage is a good illustration. It is the culmination of a rather extended process of learning, response and commitment. The first stages of a courtship may be compared to the first element in faith: content. Here each is getting to know the other, each is learning whether or not the person possesses what is needed for a good marriage. It is a very important step. If the other person cannot be trusted, for example, there will be trouble later. The second stage is comparable to the second element in faith: the movement of the heart. This corresponds to falling in love, which is quite obviously an important step beyond mere knowledge. Finally, the couple says "I do," and promises to live together and love each other regardless of what their future circumstances might be. So also we commit ourselves to Christ for this life and for eternity.

The Faith of Abraham

Faith does not stop here. As a product of the new birth, it does not disappear into the past but rather continues throughout life as a present reality. Not only does it continue, it actually grows stronger as it comes increasingly to know the nature of the one in whom it trusts.

When God called Abraham to leave Ur of the Chaldees and go into a land that he would afterward inherit, the book of Hebrews says, "Abraham obeyed . . . and he went out, not knowing where he was to go" (Heb. 11:8). This was faith, but it did not need to be strong. It was only belief in the ability of God to lead the patriarch into the land. However, Hebrews goes on to say, "By faith he sojourned in the land of promise, as in a foreign land, living in tents with Isaac and Jacob, heirs with him of the same promise" (v. 9). Faith was stronger here for it was trust in God exercised in the face of famine, danger and the delayed fulfillment of the promise. Two verses farther on, the chapter speaks of the faith through which Sarah received strength to bear a son when she was past the age of childbearing. By this point the faith of both Abraham and Sarah was very strong. It had come to know the God of the promise as the God of miracles. In reference to this event God says of Abraham in Romans, "No distrust made him waver concerning the promise of God, but he grew strong in his faith as he gave glory to God, fully convinced that God was able to do what he had promised" (Rom. 4:20-21).

We read finally that Abraham's faith conquered doubt in the midst of great emotional suffering and the seeming contradiction of all that he had previously believed. "By faith Abraham, when he was tested, offered up Isaac, and he who had received the promises was ready to offer up his only son, of whom it was said, 'Through Isaac shall your descendants be named.' He considered that God was able to raise men even from the dead; hence, figuratively speaking, he did receive him back" (Heb. 11:17-19). Abraham believed that God was able to perform a resurrection.

Such is the normal growth of faith. Your faith may be weak. Your faith may be strong. But the essential fact is that your faith is in God the Father and in his Son, our Lord Jesus Christ. God cannot fail. If you grow in your knowledge of God, you will find that your faith will also grow from strength to strength as did the faith of Abraham.

6 JUSTIFICATION BY FAITH: THE HINGE OF SALVATION

Martin Luther, whose rediscovery of the truths about justification launched the Reformation in the sixteenth century, wrote, "When the article of justification has fallen, everything has fallen." He declared, "This is the chief article from which all other doctrines have flowed." He argued, "It alone begets, nourishes, builds, preserves, and defends the church of God; and without it the church of God cannot exist for one hour." He said that it is "the master and prince, the lord, the ruler, and the judge over all kinds of doctrines."[1]

John Calvin, who followed Luther in the early development of the Reformation, said the same. He called it "the main hinge on which religion turns."[2]

Thomas Watson observed, "Justification is the very hinge and pillar of Christianity. An error about justification is dangerous, like a defect in a foundation. Justification by Christ is a spring of the water of life. To have the poison of corrupt doctrine cast into this spring is damnable."[3]

These statements are not hyperbole. They are simple truth

because justification by faith is God's answer to the most basic of all religious questions: how can a man or woman become right with God? We are not right with him in ourselves; this is the doctrine of sin. We are in rebellion against God. If we are against God, we cannot be right with God. Moreover, we are *all* transgressors, as Paul so clearly says, "All have sinned and fall short of the glory of God" (Rom. 3:23). The doctrine of justification by faith says that we may become right with God by the work of Christ alone received by faith.

Paul puts it like this: "All who believe . . . are justified by his [God's] grace as a gift" (Rom. 3:22-24); "A man is justified by faith apart from works of law" (Rom. 3:28); "To one who does not work but trusts him who justifies the ungodly, his faith is reckoned as righteousness" (Rom. 4:5). Justification is God's work. As Paul says, "It is *God* who justifies; who is to condemn?" (Rom. 8:33-34).

The Verdict of the Courts

Two points deserve emphasis. First, it is God who justifies and not we ourselves, as the quotations from Romans show. John Murray writes, "Justification is not our apology nor is it the effect in us of a process of self-excusation. It is not even our confession nor the good feeling that may be induced in us by confession. Justification is not any religious exercise in which we engage however noble and good that religious exercise may be. If we are to understand justification and appropriate its grace we must turn our thought to the action of God in justifying the ungodly."[4]

Here we are helped by the image of the salvation triangle introduced in *God the Redeemer* in a discussion of propitiation and redemption.[5] Propitiation, redemption and justification, three key words for understanding the death of Christ, may be used to connect Christ, the Father and Christians as in the diagram below.

As seen in the diagram, we are the recipients of two acts:

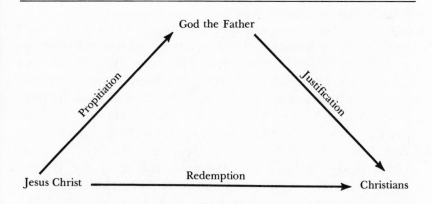

The Salvation Triangle

redemption and justification. We contribute nothing to our
salvation. Christ is the initiator of two acts: propitiation and
redemption, for it is he who achieves salvation for us. God the
Father is the recipient of one act: propitiation, Jesus satisfy-
ing God's wrath. On the basis of this the Father initiates the
last act: justification, in which he reaches out in grace to reck-
on the ungodly to be right with himself.

The second point needing emphasis is that justification is
given as a legal pronouncement, and not as a reference to
people actually becoming more holy. It is true that they will
become increasingly upright if God is actually at work in their
lives. But justification does not itself refer to this transformation. When a judge justifies someone, he does not make that
person upright or blameless. No changes are made in the person whatsoever. Rather the judge declares that in his or her
judgment the person is not guilty of the accusation that has
been made and is instead in right standing before the law that
the judge was appointed to administer. The judge is not saying anything about the accused person's character.

There is some controversy over whether or not _justification_
is used in Scripture as a legal term. But there are many rea-

sons for thinking that it is.

(1.) The Old Testament speaks strongly of God as a God of law. To the Hebrew mind this strikingly set him off from the gods of the nations round about. Moreover, because he was a God of law, he was also a God of judgment, for in a universe governed by a sovereign and moral God, evil must be punished. Abraham voiced this outlook when God told him of the pending destruction of Sodom: "Shall not the Judge of all the earth do right?" (Gen. 18:25). Here, in the early history of Israel, God is designated by the powerful term *judge*. In later writings these thoughts are elaborated. "The LORD has taken his place to contend, he stands to judge his people. The LORD enters into judgment with the elders and princes of his people" (Is. 3:13-14). "But the LORD sits enthroned for ever, he has established his throne for judgment; and he judges the world with righteousness, he judges the peoples with equity" (Ps. 9:7-8).

Justification is often linked to judgment. "Enter not into judgment with thy servant; for no man living is righteous [justified] before thee" (Ps. 143:2). "He who vindicates [justifies] me is near. Who will contend with me?" (Is. 50:8). The same idea occurs in reference to human judgment in Deuteronomy 25:1, "If there is a dispute between men, and they come into court, and the judges decide between them, acquitting [justifying] the innocent and condemning the guilty...."

(2.) Justification is contrasted with condemnation. "He who justifies the wicked and he who condemns the righteous are both alike an abomination to the LORD" (Prov. 17:15). Since condemnation does not mean to make wicked, neither can justification mean to make righteous. Both rather refer to an official decree or declaration.

(3.) Several passages use the word *justify* in reference to God being justified. For example, in Romans 3:4 Paul quotes Psalm 51:4 in saying, "Let God be true though every man be false, as it is written, 'That thou mayest be justified in thy words, and prevail when thou art judged.' " Paul does not mean that God was to be made righteous, for God is and always has been righteous. He means that in the process of judgment God's words would show that he is righteous. Similar verses are Luke 7:29 and 1 Timothy 3:16.

4. Similarly, there are passages in which people are said to justify themselves. This could mean that they were making themselves better, but the passages do not allow this reading. In Luke 16:15 Jesus says, "You are those who justify yourselves before men, but God knows your hearts." He means that they tried to declare themselves upright when actually they were not. In Luke 10:29 it is written of a young lawyer, "But he, desiring to justify himself. . . ." He tried to demonstrate that he was right in his conduct.

It would be saying too much to argue that each of these passages clearly refers to a courtroom scene. But some of them do, and the others use the word in a way that is entirely in line with this metaphorical association. There is always the idea of a judgment given and of a favorable verdict received in that judgment. Leon Morris has written, "The case is not unlike that of English verbs like 'to judge,' 'to acquit,' which are capable of being used in connection with matters far remote from law-courts, but which nevertheless are undeniably derived from legal practice and retain the essential part of their legal significance. So is it with _dikaioō_ [justify]. It may be used, it is used, in connection with matters where there is no formal giving of sentence in a law-court; but that does not alter the fact that the verb is essentially a forensic one in its biblical usage, and it denotes basically a sentence of acquittal."[6]

God Vindicated

God's judgment is always according to truth and equity. We are ungodly. How then can God justify us? If we were to declare a person who is guilty to be innocent, our act would be an outrage before both God and man. Yet this is what God does. How can he do it?

The Christian doctrine, strictly speaking, is justification *by faith* and not merely justification. Alone, justification means to declare righteous, as we have indicated. But justification by faith is God's declaring believers to be righteous not on the basis of their own works but on the basis of Christ's sacrifice. God declares that he has accepted the sacrifice of Christ as the payment of our debt to the divine justice, and in place of the sin he imputes Christ's righteousness to us.

This is the argument that Paul develops in the latter half of Romans 3:21-26. "But now the righteousness of God has been manifested apart from law, although the law and the prophets bear witness to it, the righteousness of God through faith in Jesus Christ for all who believe. For there is no distinction; since all have sinned and fall short of the glory of God, they are justified by his grace as a gift, through the redemption which is in Christ Jesus, whom God put forward as an expiation by his blood, to be received by faith. This was to show God's righteousness, because in his divine forbearance he had passed over former sins; *it was to prove at the present time that he himself is righteous and that he justifies him who has faith in Jesus*" (my emphasis).

Quite a few years ago a society for the spread of atheism prepared a tract containing half a dozen sketches of Old Testament characters combined with a lurid description of their misdeeds. No efforts were spared in describing their sin. One figure was Abraham. The leaflet pointed out that he was willing to sacrifice his wife's honor to save his own life. Yet he was called "the friend of God." The atheists asked what kind of God this is who would have a friend like Abraham. Another figure was Jacob. He was described as a cheat and a liar. Yet God called himself "the God of Jacob." Moses was portrayed as a murderer and a fugitive from justice, which he was. David was shown to be an adulterer who compounded the crime of adultery with the murder of the woman's husband. Yet David was called "a man after God's own heart." The atheists asked what kind of a God he must be who could be pleased with David.

Remarkably, this tract had hit on something which even God acknowledges. God calls himself just and holy. Yet for centuries he had been refusing to condemn and instead had actually been justifying men and women such as these. We might say that for these long centuries there had been a blot on God's name. As Paul says, he had indeed been passing over former sins. Is God unjust? No. In the death of Christ God's name and purposes are vindicated. It is now seen that on the basis of that death, God had justified and continues to justify the ungodly.

No Other Salvation

The tragedy is that people will not accept this salvation freely offered in Christ and instead attempt to earn their own salvation.

In the two chapters preceding these key verses in Romans 3, Paul puts everyone in one of three categories to show that all people need what is available only through Christ. The first category, described in Romans 1:18-32, contains people we call hedonists, those who would say, "The only standards of conduct I recognize are those I devise for myself. I therefore determine to live for myself and for whatever pleasure I find." Paul says that these people need the gospel because their way of life is leading them from God to condemnation. They may be justified in their own eyes, but this is not the justification that counts. There is still a moral law established by God, and there is still a moral God who will judge them. They must either be justified by faith in Jesus Christ or be lost.

The second category, considered in Romans 2:1-16, contains those who lead ethically superior lives. They are the moral people. They might say, "All you have said about hedonists is true. They certainly are on a path leading away from God, and they will be justly judged for it. But I am not like that. I do not live only for myself or set my own ethical standards. On the contrary, I pursue the highest moral standards I know. Therefore, your proposed solution and your call to repentance do not apply to me." Paul responds, however, that they do, for two reasons.

First, the standards of moralists, however high, still fall short of God's standards. God demands a perfection we cannot even dream of. We all understandably fall short. Second, moralists fall short even of their own standards, regardless of what they may be. Paul says, "Therefore you have no excuse, O man, whoever you are, when you judge another; for in passing judgment upon him you condemn yourself, because you, the judge, are doing the very same things" (Rom. 2:1).

What is your ethical standard? You may say, "My standard is the Sermon on the Mount." Well, do you live up to that standard? You do not, and neither does anyone else. In that sermon Jesus said, "You, therefore, must be perfect, as your heavenly Father is perfect" (Mt. 5:48), and no one is perfect. Perhaps you would answer the question by saying that your standard is the Ten Commandments. But you do not keep those either. You do not worship God wholly. You break the sabbath. You covet things that other people have. Is your standard the Golden Rule? If so, you break that, for you do not always do to others what you would like them to do to you (Mt. 7:12). Perhaps your standard is merely the lowest common denominator of human relationships: the standard of fair play. Do you achieve that? Not always! So you stand condemned by that lowest of ethical standards. Clearly, moral people must disabuse themselves of the thought that they can earn heaven. They must admit that they too need God's righteousness.

The third category, spoken of in Romans 2:17-29, is that of

<u>religious people.</u> In the context of Paul's experience these were Jews, the recipients of the law of God. They would boast of their heritage. In our day the equivalent person might say, "Yes, all the things you have said of the hedonist and the moral person are true. They are true of me. I also fall short of God's standards. But I do not put my trust there. I am religious, and so I trust God. I have been baptized and confirmed. I take communion. I give toward the church's support." Paul answers that such people need the gospel also, for all these things—though good in themselves—are inadequate. They do not affect one's standing before God. What is needed is the application of a righteousness which is not one's own but which comes from God, followed in time by an internal transformation.

What does God see when he looks at you? Does he see deeds, even religious deeds, that are not backed up by the divine life within? Or does he see his own righteousness imparted by his own sovereign act now beginning to work its way out in your conduct?

Consider Paul's own conversion. He was not a hedonist. Far from it. He was religious and moral. He trusted in what he could achieve in these areas for his salvation. He tells about it in Philippians 3:4-8: "If any other man thinks he has reason for confidence in the flesh, I have more: circumcised on the eighth day, of the people of Israel, of the tribe of Benjamin, a Hebrew born of Hebrews; as to the law a Pharisee, as to zeal a persecutor of the church, as to righteousness under the law blameless. But whatever gain I had, I counted as loss for the sake of Christ."

In the days before he met Christ his life was something like a balance sheet with assets and liabilities. He thought that being saved consisted in having more in the column of assets than in the column of liabilities. And he had considerable assets! Some he had inherited and some he had earned. Among the inherited assets was the fact that Paul had been born into a Jewish family and had been circumcised according to Jewish law on the eighth day of life. He was no proselyte, who had been circumcised in later life, nor an Ishmaelite, who was circumcised when he was thirteen years old. He was a pure-blooded Jew, born of Jewish parents ("a Hebrew born of Hebrews"). He was also an Israelite, a member of God's covenant people. Moreover, he was of the tribe of Benjamin. When civil war divided Judah from Israel after the death of Solomon, Benjamin was the one tribe that remained with Judah in the south. The northern tribes apostatized from God's revealed religion and set up schismatic altars where blood sacrifices were performed in violation of Leviticus 17. But Benjamin had remained loyal, and Paul was of that tribe.

Paul had also won advantages for himself. In regard to the law he was a Pharisee, the most faithful of all Jewish sects in their adherence to the law. He had been a zealous Pharisee, proven by his persecution of the infant church.

These were real assets from a human point of view. But the day came when Paul saw what these were in the sight of the righteous God. It was the day Jesus appeared to him on the road to Damascus. He understood that these acts of righteousness were actually like filthy rags. Before, he had said, "As to righteousness under the law [I am] blameless." Now he said, "I am the foremost of sinners" (1 Tim. 1:15). All that he had accumulated as assets were in reality not assets at all. These were liabilities that kept him from Christ. Under assets he now entered: "Jesus Christ alone."

This magnificent truth has been embodied in many hymns, including one by Augustus M. Toplady.

Nothing in my hands I bring,
Simply to thy cross I cling;
Naked, come to thee for dress;
Helpless, look to thee for grace;
Foul, I to the fountain fly;
Wash me, Savior, or I die.

Rock of Ages, cleft for me,
Let me hide myself in Thee.

The gospel says that when those who have been made alive by God, turn from their own works which can only condemn them and instead by faith embrace the Lord Jesus Christ as their Savior, God declares their sins to have been punished at Calvary and imputes the righteousness of Christ to their account.

7 JUSTIFICATION BY FAITH: THE PLACE OF WORKS

Christians are those who have been justified by God's grace through faith, not works. But does this mean that works no longer have any place in Christianity? If not, doesn't the doctrine of justification lead to immoral conduct? But if we need works, then it seems as if we must not be saved entirely by Christ after all.

Here is where Roman Catholic theology and Protestant theology part company. Although many Roman Catholics would heartily join with Protestants in affirming that justification is certainly by the grace of God through faith, they would answer the questions just posed differently from many Protestants. Some Catholics would say that works enter into justification in the sense that God justifies us in part by producing good works in us, so that we are justified by faith plus works. Protestants reply that we are justified by faith in Christ alone. Not even faith is a good work. But they add that good works must necessarily follow if we are truly justified, though they do not enter at all into justification itself.

Calvin states the truth in these words:
Why, then, are we justified by faith? Because by faith we grasp Christ's righteousness, by which alone we are reconciled to God. Yet you could not grasp this without at the same time grasping sanctification also. For he "is given unto us for righteousness, wisdom, sanctification, and redemption" (1 Cor. 1:30). Therefore Christ justifies no one whom he does not at the same time sanctify. These benefits are joined together by an everlasting and indissoluble bond, so that those whom he illumines by his wisdom, he redeems; those whom he redeems, he justifies; those whom he justifies, he sanctifies. . . . Thus it is clear how true it is that we are justified not without works yet not through works, since in our sharing in Christ, which justifies us, sanctification is just as much included in righteousness.[1]

The Church in Galatia

The book of Romans, the basis of the last chapter, deals with justification and works from the perspective of those who have not yet become believers. Because Galatians considers them in regard to those who are already believers, it should help us answer the questions we started this chapter with.

When Paul first preached to the Galatians, he had deliberately avoided any suggestion that they should conform to Jewish law, as was his custom when he presented the gospel to Gentiles. Although he taught the need for righteous conduct, salvation was to come apart from the law entirely, that is, through the death of Jesus Christ. The Galatians had believed this gospel, were baptized and had begun to live in the power of the Holy Spirit who worked miracles among them (Gal. 3:5).

Some time after this, however, the Galatians were on the verge of departing from the faith they had previously received so openly. Jewish teachers had arrived from Jerusalem, purporting to be from James, the Lord's brother. They had been teaching that Paul was wrong in his doctrine; they said that faith in Christ was not enough for salvation. The Gentiles also had to come under the law of Moses to be saved. It was not enough for them to have Christ; they must have Moses too. Specifically, the rite of circumcision must be added. The letter to the Galatians is Paul's animated response to this teaching. He had heard of at least three distinct charges from his Jewish opponents. Let me review all the charges and Paul's replies before returning to study the last two more closely.

The first charge was directed against him personally. He was not an apostle, they said. He had not been a member of Christ's band of disciples when the Lord was on earth. He had come along later. Actually, he was only an evangelist who, after he had received some small but inadequate knowledge of Christianity, turned to his own devices and produced a gospel opposed to that of the "true" apostles. This was done merely to make himself popular among the Gentiles.

Paul answers this accusation by retelling the story of his life, focusing on his relations with the other twelve apostles. Thus in Galatians 1—2 Paul shows: first, that his teaching is not dependent on other human authorities (the teaching of an apostle must come directly from God); second, that his authority had been acknowledged by the other apostles on each occasion on which they had been in contact; and last, that he had proved his own worth by standing firm for the gospel when others, including even Peter and Barnabas, had wavered.

The second charge, though closely related to the first, was theological. Since Paul was not a true apostle, it was said, his teaching was not true teaching. Paul taught that the law of Israel could be set aside, an error according to the legalizers. God's law was eternal and could not be set aside. Jesus himself had kept it. So had the disciples. If the Galatians were to be saved, they would have to keep the law too. Paul answers this charge in chapters 3 and 4, arguing from the Old Testament.

The final charge was that Paul's "false gospel" inevitably leads to loose living. Apart from law, lawlessness and immorality increase, they argued. Paul replies in Galatians 5—6 that Christianity does not lead believers away from law into nothingness but to Christ. In the person of the Holy Spirit, he comes to dwell within them and furnishes them with a new nature which alone is capable of doing what God requires. From within rather than without, the Holy Spirit produces the fruit of "love, joy, peace, patience, kindness, goodness, faithfulness, gentleness [and] self-control" (Gal. 5:22-23). Life in the Spirit is free from and above the kind of religion that would result in either legalism or license.

Given by Faith or Works?

Let us return to the second section of Paul's defense to better understand the proper place of works.

He has an interesting argument in the central chapters of the book to show that in the Christian life human works cannot perfect or complete justification. The argument is formed around the question of 3:5: "Does he who supplies the Spirit to you and works miracles among you do so by works of the law, or by hearing with faith?" How does God work? Is it by law or faith? Paul constructs a six-point argument in which he deals repeatedly first with one possibility and then another.

Point one (3:6-9) concerns Abraham. To appeal to Abraham is more than to appeal to just any historical example. It is to turn to the acknowledged father of Israel. God had called Abraham from a pagan ancestry (Josh. 24:1-2) and had established a covenant of salvation with him. It was from Abraham that the Jewish people, including Paul's legalistic opponents in Galatia, came. Jews looked back to Abraham as their father in the faith and as an example. How, then, was this important figure saved? How was Abraham justified? Paul answers by quoting Genesis 15:6. Abraham "believed

God," and "it was reckoned to him as righteousness" (Gal. 3:6).

No works entered into Abraham's justification then, and they must not enter into ours. Paul nails this conclusion down by two further observations. First, those who would be Abraham's children must be saved in the same way that their father was saved. Abraham's true children are his spiritual children, not merely those who have descended from him physically. Second, Abraham's spiritual children are not restricted in number to those who are Jews but rather include many who are Gentiles. God had proclaimed this in advance, saying that "all the nations" would be blessed in him (Gal. 3:8).

Point two of Paul's argument (3:10-14) turns to the law's own statements that, far from saving anyone, trying to follow the law condemns because all who fail to keep it in its entirety are cursed by the law. His text is Deuteronomy 27:26. Next he says no one is justified by law because the law itself teaches that we are justified by faith. His text is Habakkuk 2:4. Finally Paul says no mixture of these two principles is possible. Leviticus 18:5, he reminds us, teaches that the one beginning under the principle of law must continue under it or else abandon the law principle entirely. If there is to be hope, it must come from a different direction. Abruptly, therefore, Paul turns to the work of Christ through which the curse of the law has been exhausted and in whom all who believe find salvation.

In point three of his argument (3:15-18) Paul returns to Abraham. Even if Paul's opponents were ready to admit that Abraham was justified solely by faith, they might argue that the giving of the law at a later time changed the basis of our salvation. Otherwise, why was the law given? Paul considers the very nature of covenants to argue that nothing could change the promise made to Abraham.

In Abraham's day an oath was sometimes confirmed by a solemn ceremony in which animals were cut into two parts along the backbone and placed in two rows, the rows facing each other across a space between them. The parties to the oath walked together in the space between the rows and spoke their promises there, the promises being especially binding because of the shed blood. This was the covenant God enacted with Abraham that is described in Genesis 15. But it had this exception: God alone passed between the pieces of the animals, signifying that he alone stood behind the promises. Abraham's ability to respond to God or be faithful to God did not enter in at all. The promise was unilateral on God's part. The author of Hebrews captures this by saying, "For when God made a promise to Abraham, since he had no one greater by whom to swear, he swore by himself, saying, 'Surely I will bless you and multiply you.' And thus Abraham, having patiently endured, obtained the promise" (Heb. 6:13-15). The promise of justification through faith first made to Abraham is permanent because it is based on God's Word alone. Nothing that comes later can ever alter the solemn promises of the living God.

In point four of Paul's argument (3:19-22), he returns to the matter of law to refute the possible objection that he has actually proved too much. If what he says is true, then it would seem to follow: (1) that the law has no purpose at all in the scheme of salvation or (2) that it is actually opposed to it.

Paul answers that we have merely to understand that the law was not given by God to save humanity but rather to reveal sin so that out of a sense of sin we might turn from any legalism and instead receive the promise of faith in Jesus Christ. The law is good, but we must not mistake its purpose. In the last verse of this section Paul gives a capsule statement of the major truths of the first three chapters of Romans: the law shows that all—the hedonist, moralist, and religious person—have sinned and need a Savior, that Jesus is that Savior and that it has always been God's purpose to save a great company through him.

Point five (3:23-29) shows that, in contrast to the idea that the promise of salvation through faith is temporary, the law is temporary. "The law was our custodian until Christ came, that we might be justified by faith. But now that [the] faith has come, we are no longer under a custodian" (vv. 24-25).

In the last part of this argument (4:1-7), Paul contrasts the bondage in which believers found themselves before Christ's coming with the liberty they enjoy now.

It is easy for English readers to miss the flavor of these verses unless they realize that the moment of growing up was a specific one in antiquity involving matters of great religious and legal importance. In Judaism a boy passed from adolescence to manhood shortly after his twelfth birthday at which time he became "a son of the law." In the Greek world the minor came of age later, but there was the same emphasis on entering into full responsibility as an adult. At the festival of the _Apatouria,_ the child passed from the care of his father to the care of the state and was responsible to it.

Under Roman law there was also a time for the coming of age of a son. But the time when this took place may not have been firmly fixed. The father may have had discretion in setting the time of his son's maturity. If this is so, it leads one to think that Paul is referring primarily to the Roman custom as he observes that a child is under guardians and trustees "until the date set by the father." When the child was a minor in the eyes of the law—it is this word that Paul actually uses— his status was no different from that of a slave even though he was the future owner of a vast estate. He could make no decisions; he had no freedom. But when he reached the point in time set by his father, he entered joyfully into his new responsibility and freedom. In the same way, those who formerly were in the inferior condition of being under law, being both minors and "slaves," now should gladly enter into their new freedom and responsibility in Christ.

To do this, Paul says first that "God sent . . . his Son . . . to redeem those who were under the law, so that we might receive adoption as sons" (Gal. 4:4-5). Christ has redeemed us from slavery to sin and law so that we might be set free to serve him. Second, he says, "God . . . sent the Spirit of his Son into our hearts, crying, 'Abba! Father!' " (v. 6). Here is Paul's statement of the subjective side of salvation, the application of redemption to the individual by the work of the Holy Spirit, which we are primarily studying in this volume. Redemption by Christ is the objective work. This is the subjective. This is not something to strive after as if, having been given salvation, we must now work to achieve it on a higher level. Rather the Spirit is the gift of God to every believer simply because we are now members of his spiritual family.[2]

Life by the Spirit
Paul's conclusions follow naturally from this argument. "For freedom Christ has set us free; stand fast therefore, and do not submit again to a yoke of slavery. . . . If you receive circumcision, Christ will be of no advantage to you. . . . You are severed from Christ, you who would be justified by the law" (Gal. 5:1-2, 4). Clearly the apostle to the Gentiles is saying that if we who profess to be justified by grace through faith fall back again into law, if we get the idea that we can add to our justification in any manner by anything we have done or can do, we are actually repudiating justification by grace; we are not justified; we are still in our sins.

But does this not lead to immorality? No. Paul answers this third charge from his Jewish opponents in Galatians 5—6. Justification by the grace of God through faith is actually the only possible basis for morality. Only in this way are we set free from sin to serve God. Justification is one part of a series of acts performed by the Holy Spirit to complete our salvation. The Spirit also unites us to Christ, makes us alive in

Christ, leads us to faith and repentance, adopts us into his family and launches us into a lifetime of growth in sanctification. Because we do none of these things, because God alone does them, they must be rooted in our justification by him.

This is undoubtedly why the Holy Spirit becomes so prominent at the end of Galatians. "Through the Spirit, by faith, we wait for the hope of righteousness" (5:5). "Walk by the Spirit, and do not gratify the desires of the flesh" (5:16). "For the desires of the flesh are against the Spirit, and the desires of the Spirit are against the flesh" (5:17). "If you are led by the Spirit you are not under the law" (5:18). "The fruit of the Spirit is love, joy, peace, patience, kindness, goodness, faithfulness, gentleness, self-control" (5:22-23). "If we live by the Spirit, let us also walk by the Spirit. Let us have no self-conceit, no provoking of one another, no envy of one another" (5:25-26).

We must apply these truths on two levels. First, we must be thankful. If we are justified, we must say, "O Lord God, I thank you for a salvation like this. I am tempted to trust my works. But I recognize, painful as it may be, that I cannot attain salvation by anything I can do and instead must come to you solely on the basis of Christ's work on my behalf. It humbles me—when I think I am good. Yet it gives me hope—when I know by your own revelation to me what I really am. I thank you that you have done things in this way, because I couldn't be saved if you did not."

Second, we must look at what Paul says it means to have Christian character to see if we really are united to Christ by the work of God's Spirit. We should pray something like, "These evidences of the Spirit—love, joy, peace—are in me partially. But they are not always in me as they should be. So I ask you to work in me so that the Lord Jesus Christ, whom I serve, might be seen more clearly in my thought, speech and actions."

8 THE TESTS OF FAITH

I began this book with the stories of Cathy and Mark, two students who became Christians in very different ways but who began to ask the same question, "How can I know I'm saved?" Having considered justification in depth, it is time to return to Cathy and Mark's question and address the issue of assurance of justification directly.

Assurance is not only a question for young Christians, however. It is one that sometimes affects older Christians as well. It may arise as a perfectly normal stage in their growth in Christianity or as the result of some severe setback in life—sickness, losing a job, losing someone close through death, falling into sin. Out of a depression born of these events, Christians may ask whether they are truly God's children or whether they were merely mistaken in thinking so.

Such questions are more than a source of great concern. They can greatly effect one's Christian life. As Christians we are called to serve others as well as God. But how effective in helping others can we be if we are unsure of salvation?

When Martin Luther was wrestling through these questions, prior to the Reformation, he was a monk shut up in a monastery. Afterward, when he knew that he had been saved by Christ's death and that God had justified him, he left the monastery to launch the Reformation. How can we launch out for God if we are shut up in a monastery of doubts?

Christian Assurance

The entire book of 1 John was written to answer this question. Studying it will round off my treatment of justification begun in Romans and continued in Galatians.

The churches to which John was writing had received apostolic teaching, as had the churches of Galatia. But some time before the composition of 1 John, some members of the congregations had withdrawn to found a new fellowship (1 Jn. 2:19), no doubt claiming that their beliefs represented an improvement on what had been known before. Little is known about this defection, certainly no more than John himself tells us incidentally in this letter. But it was probably an early form of what came to be known as Gnosticism.

The Gnostics put themselves forward as "the knowing ones," the essential meaning of the word *Gnostic,* while at the same time insisting that salvation was primarily by knowledge, that is, by initiation into the mystical and allegedly superior knowledge which they possessed. In most forms of Gnosticism this meant that the importance of moral conduct was denied. Gnostics might say that they had no sin, that what they did was not sin, or that they could have fellowship with God even though they continued sinning.

Gnostics also believed that matter was inherently evil, that spirit alone was good and that there was no way to bring the two together. This accounted for the denial of the importance of the moral life, for salvation was in the realm of the spirit or mind which alone was good. It also produced a philosophical religion divorced from concrete history. For the

Gnostics a real Incarnation of the Son of God was impossible. If matter is evil, God could never have taken a human body unto himself. The Incarnation must have been in appearance only.

Apparently many of the Christians were confused by this teaching. The new teachers seemed brilliant. Were the Gnostics right? Were the old teachings to be abandoned? Had the believers been Christians all along or were their former beliefs only a preparation for this higher and more authentic form of Christianity? John answers their questions, first, by a categorical statement that Christians can and should know that they have eternal life and, second, by a presentation of three practical tests to settle the matter.

The Christian Way of Knowledge

In the letter John says clearly that his purpose is to write to Christians to show them how they can be sure they are regenerate. "I write this to you who believe in the name of the Son of God, that you may know that you have eternal life" (5:13). Other statements say, "By this we may be sure that we are in him" (2:5); "I write to you, children, because you know the Father" (2:13); "You have been anointed by the Holy One, and you all know" (2:20); "I write to you, not because you do not know the truth, but because you know it" (2:21); "Beloved, we are God's children now" (3:2); "We know that we have passed out of death into life" (3:14); "We are of the truth" (3:19); "We know that he abides in us" (3:24); "Little children, you are of God" (4:4); "By this we know that we abide in him and he in us" (4:13); "We know that we love the children of God" (5:2); "We know ... we know ... we know" (5:18-20).

Today's world puts a high premium on knowledge and the confidence it is supposed to bring. But knowledge has outstripped the ability of most persons to absorb it, except in highly specialized areas. Can a person really know anything in such circumstances? Can there be certainty? John's answer is that there can be certainty in spiritual matters. This is possible in two ways. One way, developed just preceding John's statement of purpose, is to show that God has promised justification and eternal life to any who believe on his Son. We can have assurance simply because God can be trusted.

John makes this point by contrasting divine and human testimony. "If we receive the testimony of men, the testimony of God is greater; for this is the testimony of God that he has borne witness to his Son. He who believes in the Son of God has the testimony in himself. He who does not believe God, has made him a liar, because he has not believed in the testimony that God has borne to his Son. And this is the testimony, that God gave us eternal life, and this life is in his Son. He who has the Son has life; he who has not the Son of God has not life" (5:9-12). Obviously John is trying to make the matter as clear as he possibly can. We all accept human testimony. Otherwise we would not be able to sign a contract, write a check, buy a ticket, ride a bus or do any of the thousands of other things that constitute daily living. "Well then," says John, "why should we not believe God, whose word alone is entirely trustworthy? God says that if we believe on Jesus as our Savior we are justified."

Certainty also comes in a second way. Those who believe God have an internal assurance that what they have believed is trustworthy. The Reformers termed this work of God's Spirit the *testimonium Spiritus Sancti internum*. On the other hand, those who do not believe God make him out to be a liar. They are saying that God cannot be trusted. Here the heinous nature of unbelief is evident. "Unbelief is not a misfortune to be pitied; it is a sin to be deplored. Its sinfulness lies in the fact that it contradicts the word of the one true God and thus attributes falsehood to him."[1]

In all fairness to those who doubt their salvation, it must be said that not all failures of assurance are sin in precisely this sense. To believe in Christ and yet think that God might go back on his word and not save us _is_ sin. But some know that saving faith is not mere intellectual assent to certain doctrines, that it involves commitment and trust, and they know that they have believed in Christ in some sense. But they are not sure if they have believed adequately. "Have I really trusted Christ? Have I really turned from attempts to achieve my own salvation through my own righteousness to receive Christ's righteousness instead? Have I truly been justified?"

In response to such questions John offers the three tests mentioned earlier. They are repeated in various forms throughout the letter: the _doctrinal_ test (the test of belief in Jesus Christ), the _moral_ test (the test of righteousness or obedience) and the _social_ test (the test of love).

The Doctrinal Test

A characteristic of our time, often pointed out by contemporary Christian apologists, is that people no longer strictly believe in truth. They use the term in a certain colloquial sense, referring to that which is the opposite of false. But most in the twentieth century do not mean that when a thing is said to be true it is therefore true absolutely and forever. They usually mean that it is true for some people, though perhaps not for others, or that it is true now, but not necessarily for tomorrow or the day after. This results in a great deal of uncertainty and a sense of lostness.

Christianity moves within an entirely different set of presuppositions. In this first test of the presence of new life, the doctrinal test, people begin to see things differently. Before, they doubted whether there even was such a thing as truth. Now they see that God is "true," that Christ is "the truth" and that the Bible contains "true" propositions. They do not understand it all, of course. But they do see it differently. One writer on the normal patterns of religious experience puts it like this: "Every man on whom this divine operation has passed experiences *new views of divine truth.* The soul sees in these things that which it never saw before. It discerns in the truth of God a beauty and excellence of which it had no conception until now. Whatever may be the diversity in the clearness of the views of different persons, or in the particular truths brought before the mind, they all agree in this, that there is a new perception of truth.... It is a blessed reality, and there are many witnesses of sound mind and unquestionable veracity who are ready to attest to it."[2]

John develops the doctrinal test at great length in 2:18-27 and then returns to it in 4:1-6. He quite naturally emphasizes the Gnostics' errors, primarily their denial that Jesus is the Christ. But as he states it, this error can be made by anyone. John calls it *the* lie, and the one who embraces it the liar: "Who is the liar but he who denies that Jesus is the Christ? This is the antichrist, he who denies the Father and the Son" (2:22).

When John says, "Jesus is the Christ," he does not mean merely that Jesus is the Messiah of Old Testament expectation. If he did, it would be hard to see why the Gnostics would be opposed to it. But in context John goes on to speak of Jesus as the Son, that is, as the Son of God, and of knowing the Son in the Father and the Father in the Son. In other words, John is giving a confession which includes Christ's full divinity: God became incarnate in Jesus as the Christ. The Gnostics, on the other hand, believed that the divine Christ, conceived as an emanation from the highest and superior God, came upon the man Jesus at the time of his baptism and left him before his crucifixion. This type of thinking is not foreign to some forms of modern biblical criticism which drive a wedge between what is called the historical Jesus and the Christ of faith.

This basic confession of the apostle John also includes all that the Father has said about Jesus in the Bible. Calvin writes,

I readily agree with the ancients, who thought that Derinthus and Carpocrates are here referred to. But the denial of Christ extends much further; for it is not enough to confess in one word that Jesus is the Christ, but he must be acknowledged to be such as the Father offers him to us in the Gospel. The two I mentioned gave the title of Christ to the Son of God, but imagined he was a mere man. Others followed, like Arius, who adorned him with the name of God but despoiled him of his eternal divinity. Marcion dreamed that he was a mere phantom. Sabellius imagined that he differed in nothing from the Father. All these denied the Son of God, for none of them really acknowledged the whole Christ, but adulterated the truth about him so far as they were able and made for themselves an idol instead of Christ....

We now see that Christ is denied whenever the things that belong to him are taken from him. And as Christ is the end of the Law and the Gospel and has within himself all the treasures of wisdom and understanding, so also is he the mark at which all heretics aim and direct their arrows. Therefore, the apostle has good reason to make those who fight against Christ the leading liars, since the full truth is exhibited to us in him. [3]

To confess that Jesus is the Christ is to confess the Christ of the Scriptures. To deny *that* Christ, by whatever means, is heresy —a heresy with terrible consequences.

For one thing, to deny the Son is to deny the Father. No doubt the false teachers would have pretended to be worshiping the same God as the Christians. "We only differ from you in your views about Jesus," they might have said. But John says that this is impossible. If Jesus is God, to deny Jesus as God is to deny God. Second, to deny the Son is to forfeit the presence of God in one's life or, as we could also say, to have no part of him or he of us. John uses the phrase "has the Father" (2:23). In biblical language this is equivalent to saying that such people remain unregenerate and under God's just condemnation. Those who confess Christ have found the Father and have been justified by him.

The Moral Test

The moral test is cited in 1 John 2:3-6 and 3:4-10 and alluded to at other points in the letter. Simply put, those who know God will increasingly lead righteous lives. It does not mean that they will be sinless. But they will be moving in a direction marked out by the righteousness of God. If this does not happen, if they are not increasingly dissatisfied with and distressed by sin, they are not God's children. "He who says 'I know him' but disobeys his commandments is a liar, and the truth is not in him; but whoever keeps his word, in him truly love for God is perfected. By this we may be sure that we are in him" (2:4-5).

In these verses John introduces two types of people, those who claim to know God but who do not keep his commandments and those who obey God out of a genuine love of him. John has harsh words for the first group. He calls them liars, for they are neither deceived by others nor confused by facts. Rather, they openly profess something which they know is not true. When John goes on to say, "The truth is not in him," he may be adding advice that others should not seek truth in such people but should go to another source. If so, the phrase applies to the false teachers (whom true seekers after God should avoid) of John's day and in our time. Truth should be sought not from those who only have intellectual qualifications but from those whose claim to spiritual knowledge is backed by godlike conduct.

The second group, those who obey God, have love for God perfected in them. Though they may make no great claims to know God, as the Gnostics did, John says they still know God.

Some years ago when the so-called new morality was at its peak, a number of theologians met at Princeton Theological Seminary to discuss it. Most were in favor. So the discussion centered on the value of being free of all rules and regulation. "But there must be some guidelines," someone said. This was discussed. At length it was decided that the only acceptable guideline was love. Anything that flowed from love was permissible, so long as it did not hurt anybody. While the discussion was proceeding along these lines a Roman Catholic priest became very quiet. At length it was noticeable. The others turned to him and asked what he thought. "Don't you agree that the only limiting factor in any ethical decision is love?" The priest replied, "If you love me, you will keep my commandments' " (Jn. 14:15).

Do we say we are Christians? Then, "He who says he abides in him ought to walk in the same way in which he walked" (1 Jn. 2:6). The call is to emulate the Lord Jesus Christ in our conduct. To walk as Christ walked is to live not by rules but by example. It is to follow him, to be his disciple. A disciple like this is personal, active and costly.

It is personal because it cannot be passed off on another. Indeed, we are to find ourselves with Christ, as Peter did following the resurrection. Jesus asked Peter, "Do you love me?" When Peter replied "Yes," he was told, "Feed my sheep." This was repeated twice more, and the repetition began to irritate Peter. So, to escape Christ's careful probing he pointed to the beloved disciple, who was apparently standing some distance away, and asked, "Lord, what about this man?" Jesus replied, "If it is my will that he remain until I come, what is that to you? Follow me!" There was no escaping the call to personal discipleship for Peter. To walk as Christ walked is also active because the Lord himself is active. To be inactive is to be left behind. Finally, it is costly because the path that Jesus walked, though it leads to glory, is the path to crucifixion first. Such a path can only be walked by those who have died to self and have deliberately taken up the cross of Christ to follow him.

Such people, whether in John's day or our own, will always have confidence before God and will be sure that they know him. Here C. H. Dodd, former professor of New Testament at the University of Cambridge, concludes,

In this passage our author is not only rebutting dangerous tendencies in the church of his time, but discussing a problem of perennial importance, that of the validity of religious experience. We may have the feeling of awareness of God, of union with him, but how shall we know that such experience corresponds to reality? It is clear that no amount of clearness or strength in the experience itself can guarantee its validity, any more than the extreme vividness of a dream leads us to suppose that it is anything but a dream. If, however, we accept the revelation of God in Christ, then we must believe that any experience of God which is valid has an ethical quality defined by what we know of Christ. It will carry with it a renewed fidelity to his teaching and example. The writer does not mean that only those who perfectly obey Christ and follow his example can be said to have experience of God. That would be to affirm the sinlessness of Christians in a sense which he has repudiated. But unless the experience includes a setting of the affections and will in the direction of the moral principles of the Gospel, it is no true experience of God, in any Christian sense. [4]

There is more to be said, of course, but thus far the test of one's experience holds. By the test of righteousness we may know that we know God and may assure our hearts before him.

The Social Test

In the midst of his final discourses before his crucifixion Jesus imparted a new commandment, the command to love. "A new commandment I give to you, that you love one another; even as I have loved you, that you also love one another. By this all men will know that you are my disciples, if you have love for one another" (Jn. 13:34-35). Love is the mark by which the world may know that Christians truly are Christians. In 1 John the command is repeated, but with this difference: it is by love that *Christians* (as well as the world) may know that they are Christians. That is, when Christians find themselves beginning to love and actually loving those others for whom Christ died, they can be assured that they know God. John develops this test in 2:7-11 and repeats it both in 3:11-18 and 4:7-21. John's clearest statement of this test is in 2:9-10: "He who says he is in the light and hates his brother is in the darkness still. He who loves his brother abides in the light, and in it there is no cause for stumbling."

As in the moral test, these verses also contain two specific groups to make the test concrete. The first group is typified by the person who "says he is in the light and hates his brother." Such people are in darkness. Clearly John is thinking of his Gnostic opponents who claimed to be the "enlightened" ones. But the same is true of any who profess regeneration without this change. Paul said essentially the same thing: "If I have prophetic powers, and understand all mysteries and all knowledge, and if I have all faith, so as to remove mountains, but have not love, I am nothing" (1 Cor. 13:2).

John's second group are those who show that they abide in the light by loving fellow Christians. John says that there is "no cause for stumbling" in their behavior. The idea of stumbling may be applied to those who not only walk in the light themselves but who also do not cause others to trip in the dark. Again, stumbling can apply to those who walk in the light and therefore do not stumble. The context almost demands this second explanation, for the point of the verses is not what happens to others but the effect of love and hate on individuals themselves. The negative equivalent of this statement occurs just one verse later. "But he who hates his brother is in the darkness and walks in the darkness, and does not know where he is going, because the darkness has blinded his eyes" (1 Jn. 2:11).

This last verse introduces the term _walk_ which may be applied to the life of love. It suggests practical steps. Love is not a certain benign feeling nor a smile. It is an attitude which determines what we do. It is impossible to speak meaningfully of love in the Christian sense without speaking of the actions which flow from it, just as it is impossible to speak meaning-fully of God's love without mentioning such things as the creation, the giving of the Old Testament revelation, the coming of Christ, the cross and the outpouring of the Holy Spirit.

What will happen if those who profess the life of Christ actually love one another? Francis Schaeffer has several suggestions. First, when a Christian has failed to love another Christian and has acted wrongly toward that person, the believer will go and apologize. This expresses love and re-stores that oneness which Jesus said should flow from Chris-tians loving one another. It verifies their Christianity before the world.

Second, when someone else hurts us, we are to show our love by forgiveness. This is hard, particularly when the other person does not say "I am sorry." Schaeffer writes, "We must all continually acknowledge that we do not practice the for-giving heart as we should. And yet the prayer is, 'Forgive us our debts, our trespasses, as we forgive our debtors.' We are to have a forgiving spirit even before the other person ex-presses regret for his wrong. The Lord's prayer does not suggest that when the other man is sorry, then we are to show a oneness by having a forgiving spirit. Rather, we are called upon to have a forgiving spirit without the other man having made the first step. We may still say that he is wrong, but in the midst of saying that he is wrong, we must be forgiving."[5]

Early in John's own life he was known as one of the "sons of thunder." He once wanted to call down fire from heaven upon those who rejected Jesus (Lk. 9:54). But as he came to know more about God, he called for love among the brethren.

Third, we must show love even when it is costly. Love cost the Samaritan in Christ's parable. It cost him time and money. Love cost the shepherd who endured hardship to hunt for his sheep. Love cost Mary of Bethany who, out of her love, broke the box of valuable ointment over the feet of Jesus. Love will be costly to all who practice it. But what is purchased by such love will be of great value. It will be proof of the presence of the life of God both to the individual Christian and to the watching world.

9

A NEW FAMILY

In the opening pages of *A Place for You,* the noted Swiss psychologist Paul Tournier tells of a young man he once counseled. He grew up in a religious home, but it was unhappy. Eventually there was a divorce. This produced unfortunate psychological symptoms in the young man's life. He developed an acute sense of failure, first in not reconciling his parents, then in his studies, then in an inability to settle down and achieve in any area of life. At last he came to see Tournier. They talked, and on one occasion, as if summing up his thought, the young man explained, "Basically, I'm always looking for a place—for somewhere to be."[1]

The need for a place is virtually universal. On the human level the principle is easy to discern. "The child who has been able to grow up harmoniously in a healthy home finds a welcome everywhere. In infancy all he needs is a stick placed across two chairs to make himself a house, in which he feels quite at home. Later on, wherever he goes, he will be able to make any place his own, without any effort on his part. For him it will not be a matter of seeking, but of choosing." On the other hand, "when the family is such that the child cannot fit himself into it properly, he looks everywhere for some other place, leading a wandering existence, incapable of settling down anywhere. His tragedy is that he carries about within himself this fundamental incapacity for any real attachment."[2] On the spiritual level, the problem is detected in the alienation from God we feel as a result of the Fall and of our own deliberate sins. Saint Augustine once wrote, "Thou hast formed us for thyself. . . . " That is our true place. But he added in frank recognition of our dilemma and sin, "And our hearts are restless till they find rest in Thee."[3]

God has dealt with this great problem of alienation through adoption, taking a person from one family (or no family) and placing him or her in a new family—the family of God. Sometimes adoption has been thought of merely as one aspect of justification or as only another way of stating what happens in regeneration. But adoption is nevertheless much more than either of these other acts of grace. "Justification means our acceptance with God as righteous and the bestowal of the title to everlasting life. Regeneration is the renewing of our hearts after the image of God. But these blessings in themselves, however precious they are, do not indicate what is conferred by the act of adoption. By adoption the redeemed become sons and daughters of the Lord God Almighty; they are introduced into and given the privileges of God's family."[4]

Only adoption suggests the new family relationship which is ours in Christ and points to the privileges of that relationship. "For all who are led by the Spirit of God are sons of God. For you did not receive the spirit of slavery to fall back into fear, but you have received the spirit of sonship. When we cry, 'Abba! Father!' it is the Spirit himself bearing witness with our spirit that we are children of God, and if children, then heirs, heirs of God and fellow heirs with Christ, provided we suffer with him in order that we may also be glorified with him" (Rom. 8:14-17).

These verses speak of adoption as a separate work of God's Spirit through which: (1) we are delivered from bondage to the law and from fear; (2) we are assured of our new relationship to God; and (3) we become God's heirs with Christ.

Murray also writes,

1. Though adoption is distinct it is never separable from justification and regeneration. The person who is justified is always the recipient of sonship. And those who are given the right to become sons of God are those who, as John 1:13 indicates, "were born not of blood nor of the will of the flesh nor of the will of man but of God." 2. Adoption is, like justification, a judicial act. In other words, it is the bestowal of a status, or standing, not the generating within us of a new nature or character. It concerns a relationship and not the attitude or disposition which enables us to recognize and cultivate that relationship. 3. Those adopted into God's family are also given the Spirit of adoption whereby they are able to recognize their sonship and exercise the privileges which go with it. "And because ye are sons, God hath sent forth the Spirit of his Son into your hearts, crying Abba, Father" (Gal. 4:6; cf. Rom. 8:15, 16). The Spirit of adoption is the consequence but this does not itself constitute adoption. 4. There is a close relationship between adoption and regeneration.[5]

The relationship is explained by the way a father in ancient times would officially adopt his own son as his legal representative and heir. As we indicated in chapter seven, in a discussion of Galatians 4:1-7, this was an important moment in the coming of age of a Jewish, Greek or Roman child. Before, he was a son by birth. Now he became a son legally and passed from the care of his guardian or trustee into manhood. Although in Christian experience regeneration and adoption take place simultaneously, adoption nevertheless emphasizes the Christian's new status while regeneration emphasizes the newness of life.

New Relationships

Perhaps the words *new status* are not the best. What is really involved in adoption is *new relationships:* a new relationship to God and a new relationship to other people within the household of faith.

The new relationship to God need not have been automatic. Having justified us, God could still have left us on a much inferior level of status and privilege. Instead, he took us into his own family giving us the status and privilege of daughters and sons. So great is God's condescension in this act of adoption that we would be inclined to dismiss it, thinking it presumption, were it not that God has made a special effort to seal these truths to our hearts. As Paul wrote, " 'What no eye has seen, nor ear heard, nor the heart of man conceived, what God has prepared for those who love him,' God has revealed to us through the Spirit. For the Spirit searches everything, even the depths of God" (1 Cor. 2:9-10).

There is a certain (unbiblical) sense in which God may be said to be the Father of all. God is the creator of all. He sustains our lives moment by moment, for "in him we live and move and have our being" (Acts 17:28; compare vv. 24-28). On account of this we may be said to be "God's offspring" (v. 29). But there are no privileges attached to this more general "fatherhood." The relationship which the word properly describes is missing.

Jesus taught quite pointedly that some who thought they were God's children were, according to his teaching, actually children of the devil. After saying, "And you will know the truth, and the truth will make you free," the Jews answered him, "We are descendants of Abraham, and have never been in bondage to any one. How is it that you say, 'You will be made free'?" Jesus responded, "I know that you are descendants of Abraham; yet you seek to kill me.... If you were Abraham's children, you would do what Abraham did." At this point the people grew angry and accused him of being illegitimate. Then in righteous anger the Lord replied, "If God were your Father, you would love me, for I proceeded and came forth from God; I came not of my own accord, but he sent me. Why do you not understand what I say? It is because you cannot bear to hear my word. You are of your father the devil, and your will is to do your father's desires" (Jn. 8:32-33, 37, 39, 42-44). In this exchange Jesus put to an end the misleading doctrine that God is the Father of all and all are his children.

But it is not only that Christians have a new relationship to God as a result of his act of adoption. We also have a new relationship with one another which requires us to love each other and work together as befits brothers and sisters. Before, we were outside the family of God, each going our own way in opposition to and sometimes in only thinly veiled hostility toward each other. Now we are different: "So then you are no longer strangers and sojourners, but you are fellow citizens with the saints and members of the household of God" (Eph. 2:19).

The attitudes that should flow from these new relationships do not always follow naturally or easily. But that is all the more reason to grasp this truth forcefully and work at the relationships. John White has put the task in these terms,

> _You were cleansed by the same blood, regenerated by the same Spirit. You are a citizen of the same city, a slave of the same master, a reader of the same Scriptures, a worshiper of the same God. The same presence dwells silently in you as in them. Therefore you are committed to them and they to you. They are your brothers, sisters, your fathers, mothers and children in God. Whether you like or dislike them, you belong to them. You have responsibilities toward them that must be discharged in love. As long as you live on this earth, you are in their debt. Whether they have done much or little for you, Christ has done all. He demands that your indebtedness to him be transferred to your new family._ [6]

Membership in God's family does not mean that we will be

insensitive to its human faults. Indeed, we must be sensitive to them if we are to have any hope of eliminating them and improving the quality of our family relationships. But neither should we be overly sensitive to the faults of our brothers and sisters in Christ. Even less should we be openly critical. We should be intensely committed to each other with a proper family loyalty and work to help each other in living the Christian life. We should pray for each other and serve one another.

Family Privileges

Our new relationships give us new privileges. Some we have now. Some pertain more fully to the life we will enjoy in heaven. These latter privileges are described in Scripture as our inheritance. We are not told specifically what they are, though they obviously involve the possession of the life of heaven and other blessings. Our inheritance is described as spiritual "riches" (Eph. 1:18) and as a "reward" for faithful service (Col. 3:24). It is said to be "eternal" (Heb. 9:15). Peter declares that by the mercy of God "we have been born anew to a living hope through the resurrection of Jesus Christ from the dead, and to an inheritance which is imperishable, undefiled, and unfading, kept in heaven for you" (1 Pet. 1:3-4). Paul describes the Holy Spirit as a present "guarantee" of what awaits us (Eph. 1:14).

Prayer is the key privilege of adoption which we enjoy now. On the one hand, this is described as a consequence of our justification. "Therefore, since we are justified by faith, we have peace with God through our Lord Jesus Christ. Through him we have obtained access to this grace in which we stand" (Rom. 5:1-2). *Access* means access to God. On the other hand, access is based on our adoption. Because of it we can approach God as "Father." And only through the Spirit of adoption can we be assured that God is our Father and that he indeed hears our prayers. This is what Paul is speaking of in the verse

A New Family 113

quoted earlier. "When we cry, 'Abba! Father!' it is the Spirit himself bearing witness with our spirit that we are children of God" (Rom. 8:15-16).

Our authority to call God "Father" goes back to Jesus Christ himself and to no less important a statement than the opening phrases of the Lord's Prayer. "Pray then like this: Our Father who art in heaven..." (Mt. 6:9). No Old Testament Jew ever addressed God directly as "my Father." The invocation of the Lord's Prayer was something new and startlingly original to Christ's contemporaries. This has been documented by the late German scholar, Ernst Lohmeyer, in a book called *"Our Father"* and by the contemporary biblical scholar Joachim Jeremias in an essay entitled "Abba" and a booklet called *The Lord's Prayer*.[7] According to these scholars three things are indisputable: (1) the title was new with Jesus; (2) Jesus always used this form of address in praying; and (3) Jesus authorized his disciples to use the same word after him.

It is true, of course, that in one sense the title *father* for God is as old as religion. Homer wrote of "Father Zeus, who rules over the gods and mortal men." Aristotle explained that Homer was right because "paternal rule over children is like that of a king over his subjects" and "Zeus is king of us all." In this case the word *father* means "Lord." The point to notice, however, is that the address was always impersonal. In Greek thought God was called father in the same sense that a king is called a father of his country.

The Old Testament uses the word *father* as a designation of God's relationship to Israel, but even this is not personal. Nor is it frequent. In fact, it occurs only fourteen times in the whole of the Old Testament. Israel is called the "first-born son" of God (Ex. 4:22). David says, "As a father pities his children, so the LORD pities those who fear him" (Ps. 103:13). Isaiah writes, "Yet, O LORD, thou art our Father" (Is. 64:8). But in none of these passages does any individual

Israelite address God directly as "my Father." In most of them the point is that Israel has not lived up to the family relationship. Thus, Jeremiah reports the Lord as saying, "I thought how I would set you among my sons, and give you a pleasant land, a heritage most beauteous of all nations. And I thought you would call me, My Father, and would not turn from following me. Surely, as a faithless wife leaves her husband, so have you been faithless to me, O house of Israel, says the LORD" (Jer. 3:19-20).

In the time of Jesus the distance between people and God seemed to be widening. The names of God were increasingly withheld from public speech and prayers. This trend was completely overturned by Jesus. He always called God Father, and this fact must have impressed itself in an extraordinary way upon the disciples. Not only do all four of the Gospels record that Jesus used this address, but they report that he did so in all his prayers (Mt. 11:25; 26:39, 42; Mk. 14:36; Lk. 23:34; Jn. 11:41; 12:27; 17:1, 5, 11, 21, 24-25). The only exception enforces its own significance, the cry from the cross: "My God, my God, why hast thou forsaken me?" (Mt. 27:46; Mk. 15:34). That prayer was wrung from Christ's lips at the moment in which he was made sin for mankind and in which the relationship he had with his Father was temporarily broken. At all other times Jesus boldly assumed a relationship to God that was thought to be highly irreverent or blasphemous by most of his contemporaries.

This is of great significance for our prayers. Jesus was the Son of God in a unique sense, and God was uniquely his Father. He came to God in prayer as God's unique Son. Now he reveals that this same relationship can be true for those who believe in him, whose sins are removed by his suffering. They can come to God as God's children. God can be their own individual Father.

But this is not all. When Jesus addressed God as Father he did not use the normal word for father. He used the Aramaic word *abba*. Obviously this was so striking to the disciples that they remembered it in its Aramaic form and repeated it in Aramaic even in their Greek Gospels and other writings. Mark uses it in his account of Christ's prayer in Gethsemane, "Abba, Father, all things are possible to thee" (Mk. 14:36). Paul also makes note of it in the verses to which we referred earlier (Rom. 8:15; Gal. 4:6).

What does *abba* specifically mean? The early church fathers —Chrysostom, Theodor of Mopsuestia and Theodore of Cyrrhus, who came from Antioch (where Aramaic was spoken and who probably had Aramaic-speaking nurses—unanimously testify that *abba* was the address of small children to their fathers.[8] The Talmud confirms this when it says that when a child is weaned "it learns to say *abba* and *imma*" (that is, "daddy" and "mommy").[9] That is what *abba* means: daddy. To a Jewish mind a prayer addressing God as daddy would not only have been improper, it would have been irreverent to the highest degree. Yet this was what Jesus said, and this quite naturally stuck in the minds of the disciples, as I have indicated. It was something quite new and unique when Jesus instructed his disciples to call God daddy.

Confidence in Our Father

This gives us assurance as we stand before God. When we approach God as Father, being taught and led to do so by God's own Spirit, we know that we stand in a secure relationship.

Is God our Father? If he is, then he will help us in the days of our infancy, teaching us to walk spiritually and picking us up when we fall down. This is why Hosea could report God as saying, "Yet it was I who taught Ephraim to walk, I took them up in my arms. . . . I led them with cords of compassion, with the bands of love. . . . How can I give you up, O Ephraim! How can I hand you over, O Israel!" (Hos. 11:3-4, 8). A God like this will keep us from falling and will present us "without blemish before the presence of his glory" (Jude 24).

Is God our Father? Then he will care for us through the days of this life and will bless us abundantly. The laws of the United States recognize that parents must care for their children. So does God. He has set down the rule that "children ought not to lay up for their parents, but parents for their children" (2 Cor. 12:14). If this is true on the human level, it is also true of the relationship of a person to God. The Lord Jesus said, "Do not be anxious about your life, what you shall eat or what you shall drink, nor about your body, what you shall put on. . . . Do not be anxious, saying, 'What shall we eat?' or 'What shall we drink?' or 'What shall we wear?' For the Gentiles seek all these things; and your heavenly Father knows that you need them all. But seek first his kingdom and his righteousness, and all these things shall be yours as well" (Mt. 6:25, 31-33).

Is God our Father? Then he will go before us to show the way through this life. Paul alludes to this when he writes, "Therefore be imitators [followers] of God, as beloved children" (Eph. 5:1).

Is God our Father? Then we shall know that we belong to him forever. We shall know that while we are being led, taught and educated for life's tasks, nothing shall interfere with his purpose for us in Christ. We shall look forward to the time when we shall see him and be like him, for we shall see him as he is.

10 THE UPWARD WAY

One of the early signs of the saving work of God in the life of an individual is dissatisfaction with sin and a striving for holiness. But neither dissatisfaction on the one hand nor striving on the other is the same as holiness itself. Holiness is a goal toward which we move.

If we do not think of holiness in the strongest biblical terms, but rather in our own, we may imagine that we have attained perfection and may even become complacent in the Christian life. If we understand it biblically, we instead find ourselves being thrown back on the power of the Holy Spirit to work in us. Sanctification, which is the proper word for this aspect of the Spirit's work in believers, describes two basic areas of growth. The first is separation to God and his purposes. For the root meaning of holiness suggests that which has been "set apart" to God. The second is God-pleasing conduct or morality, becoming more like Jesus. We will increasingly think as he would think and act as he would act.

This goal of holiness then has an outward standard of

morality coupled with an internal conformity to the will and mind of God. Though there are negative implications, sanctification is a positive desire for and actual growth in Christian character.

Perfect, Yet Being Perfected

We are still sinners even though regenerated and justified in God's sight. Although we are perfect in terms of our present standing before God, we are far from perfect in our actual thoughts and conduct. Sanctification aims to close this gap. Paul was aware of this when he wrote to the Philippians, "Not that I have already obtained this or am already *perfect;* but I press on to make it my own, because Christ Jesus has made me his own" (Phil. 3:12). Then, just three verses later he continues, "Let those of us who are mature [the Greek word is the same—perfect] be thus minded" (v. 15). Clearly, although Paul knew that his record had already been cleared before God on the basis of Christ's work and although he had attained maturity in the Christian life, he was also aware of the necessary growth in holiness that lay before him.

All Christians have this experience. When we first believe in Jesus as Savior, most of us have a great sense of joy and gratitude to God for salvation. In this grateful state of mind we often feel that everything has changed. We are liberated from sin. We are new creatures in Christ. But actually, we are not much different in natural inclinations, character and conduct. Before, we had bad habits. Now we are saved, but many of these bad habits and wrong actions remain. Should we doubt the reality of salvation? Not at all. The very fact that we are now aware of these imperfections in a new way is proof that God's work of transformation has begun. Instead of discouragement or doubt, we should realize that we have entered on a new way of life in which many former patterns must change. As God works there will be an increasing distaste for sin and a growing hunger for righteousness.

Because sanctification is a process which is never completed in this world does not mean it is of secondary importance or (even worse) dispensable. It is as important and necessary in the application of salvation as regeneration, justification and adoption. John Murray stresses the gravity of sanctification by three statements: (1) all sin in believers is the contradiction of God's holiness; (2) the presence of sin in believers involves conflict in their hearts and lives; and (3) though sin still remains it does not have the mastery.[1]

The first statement is drawn from such passages as 1 Peter 1:15-16 ("But as he who called you is holy, be holy yourselves in all your conduct; since it is written, 'You shall be holy, for I am holy' "), 1 John 2:16 ("The lust of the flesh and the lust of the eyes and the pride of life, is not of the Father but is of the world") and 1 John 3:2-3 ("Beloved, we are God's children now; it does not yet appear what we shall be, but we know that when he appears we shall be like him, for we shall see him as he is. And every one who thus hopes in him purifies himself as he is pure"). If we are God's children we should be like him in holiness as well as in other aspects of his character.

Romans 7 is a classic example of the conflict that exists in the believer's life when sin is present—the second of Murray's statements. "I do not understand my own actions. For I do not do what I want, but I do the very thing I hate. . . . When I want to do right, evil lies close at hand. For I delight in the law of God, in my inmost self, but I see in my members another law at war with the law of my mind and making me captive to the law of sin which dwells in my members" (Rom. 7:15, 21-23).

It is futile to argue that this conflict is not normal. If there is still sin to any degree in one who is indwelt by the Holy Spirit, then there is tension, yes, contradiction, within the heart of that person. Indeed, the more sanctified the person is, the more conformed he is to the image of his Savior, the more he must recoil against every lack of conformity to the holiness of God. The deeper his apprehension of *the majesty of God, the greater the intensity of his love to God, the more persistent his yearning for the attainment of the prize of the high calling of God in Christ Jesus, the more conscious will he be of the gravity of the sin which remains and the more poignant will be his detestation of it. The more closely he comes to the holiest of all, the more he apprehends the sinfulness that is his and he must cry out, "O wretched man that I am" (Rom. 7:24). Was this not the effect in all the people of God as they came into closer proximity to the revelation of God's holiness? "Woe is me! for I am undone, because I am a man of unclean lips, and I dwell in the midst of a people of unclean lips; for mine eyes have seen the King, the Lord of hosts" (Is. 6:5). "I have heard of thee by the hearing of the ear; but now mine eye seeth thee. Wherefore I abhor myself, and repent in dust and ashes" (Job 42:5, 6).*[2]

The third of Murray's points, that although sin remains it is not the master, is taught in the very next verses of Romans: "The law of the Spirit of life in Christ Jesus has set me free from the law of sin and death. For God has done what the law, weakened by the flesh, could not do: sending his own Son in the likeness of sinful flesh and for sin, he condemned sin in the flesh, in order that the just requirement of the law might be fulfilled in us, who walk not according to the flesh but according to the Spirit" (8:2-4).

While sanctification is important from the perspective of our own fulfillment as Christians, its importance is seen even more when measured against these three statements. If we were to say that becoming more holy is unnecessary, that we will simply remain in known sin, then we are effectively saying that God is not holy, that sin does not involve a contradiction and conflict in us, and that God has not made provision for victory. In each case we are denying Scripture and calling God a liar.

We should, of course, turn from sin and seek God's help, strength and encouragement to live the holy life we desperately need.

Let Go or Get Going?

This way of speaking raises a difficult question, however. Who accomplishes sanctification? This would seem to be the work of God's Spirit. We read in 1 Thessalonians 5:23, "May the God of peace himself sanctify you wholly." Again, in 2 Corinthians 3:18-19, "And we all, with unveiled face, beholding the glory of the Lord, are being changed into his likeness from one degree of glory to another; for this comes from the Lord who is the Spirit." There are scores of such references. People who emphasize these Scriptures speak of "letting go" of ourselves and "letting God" do the work of sanctification in us.

But there are other verses that speak of *our* role in sanctification. We are told, "Walk by the Spirit, and do not gratify the desires of the flesh" (Gal. 5:16). "Be imitators of God, as beloved children" (Eph. 5:1). "Put on the whole armor of God, that you may be able to stand against the wiles of the devil" (Eph. 6:11). People who emphasize these verses speak of our obligation to use these "means of grace" available to us.

Which of these is right and which is wrong? If we mean by "letting go" that we may therefore abandon Bible study, prayer, Christian fellowship and the worship of God and still expect to grow in the Christian life just because we have "let go," we are greatly mistaken. We will stagnate in the Christian life and drift away from Christian circles. But we are also wrong if we think that by making use of these means we can automatically achieve our own sanctification. The correct understanding is a combination of the two, working as fully and consistently as possible: God working in us and we being as diligent and obedient as possible in these areas.

If there was ever a point to stop and merely rejoice in the wonders of what God is doing in Christ, to sit back and let God work, it is certainly after the hymn of praise to Christ found in Philippians 2:5-11. But Paul does not allow us to do this. Instead he immediately applies the doctrine saying, "Therefore, my beloved, as you have always obeyed, so now, not only as in my presence but much more in my absence, work out your own salvation with fear and trembling; for God is at work in you, both to will and to work for his good pleasure" (Phil. 2: 12-13). He does not mean, "Work for your salvation." He means, "Since you are saved, since God has already entered your life in the person and power of his Holy Spirit and is at work within you conforming you to the image of the Lord Jesus Christ—because of these things you are now to work as hard as you can to express the fullness of this great reality in your conduct. Nevertheless, as you do this, it is God who does the working."

Peter said the same thing. "[God's] divine power has granted to us all things that pertain to life and godliness. . . ." It is all of God. Nevertheless, Peter continues, "For this very reason make every effort to supplement your faith with virtue, and virtue with knowledge, and knowledge with self-control, and self-control with steadfastness, and steadfastness with godliness, and godliness with brotherly affection, and brotherly affection with love" (2 Pet. 1:3, 5-7).

John White concludes correctly, "Let there be no misunderstanding. Without God's Spirit within, our efforts are futile. No good thing could spring from our corrupt and sinful hearts. But we have been redeemed and we have been sanctified. We have been set apart for God's use. Let us then agree with God in the matter. . . . Let us assume the whole armor of God and by miraculous strength declare war on all that is evil within and without."[3] This is not optional. We are commanded to do this, and there is no point in our Christian lives when we are more conscious of the power of God's Spirit within than when we obey. We can hardly expect to grow spiritually if we will not use that spiritual food and drink which God puts at our disposal.

The Means of Grace

The next part of this book will discuss the primary means of grace: prayer, Bible study and Christian service. But there are others as well, and it is worth considering them together. There are at least seven.

1. Assurance. We have already touched on this matter in the chapter on how we may know we are justified. But it can also help us grow toward Christlike character. Luther once put the matter graphically: "A wavering heart that does not firmly believe and hold that it will receive something will certainly get nothing, because God cannot give it anything, much as he would like to. Such a heart is like a vessel which a man holds in his hands but, instead of holding it, constantly moves it to and fro. It will be impossible to pour anything into it, and though you would want to do so, you would miss the vessel and waste whatever you are pouring. So it is with a wavering, unbelieving heart. God would like to give what we need. But there we stand, like a foolish beggar, holding out our hat for gifts and yet not holding it still."[4]

Assurance is the first necessary item in sanctification because it is a matter of taking God at his word and of knowing that he has truly begun a work of salvation in us. If we have believed God here, we can believe him in other matters. If we are sure that we have really begun our journey, we can then get on with it as quickly and efficiently as possible.

2. Knowledge. Knowing everything is not essential for sanctification, but knowing the basics will certainly help. One writer has said, "As assurance is the practical foundation . . . so knowledge of our position in Christ is the practical road that leads to experimental holiness."[5]

What truths should Christians know to grow in the Christian life? Some key ones are set forth in the earlier chapters of this book: the person of the Holy Spirit and his work; God's initiative in bringing us to faith in Christ; the Spirit's ministry in uniting us to Christ, from which comes our new status before God; our access to God through prayer; our security in Christ. If we know what our new status is, we can take advantage of its privileges. If we know God hears us, we can depend on the Holy Spirit to help us pray and interpret our stammering prayers. If we are secure in Christ, although we may stumble and fall, we know that nothing will ever pluck us out of Christ's hand.

3. Bible study. The Bible as a source of growth in the Christian life is linked to assurance and knowledge, for from the Bible we gain both. But the Bible as a means of grace is more than either. In Bible study we seek to know God personally. Here God consistently and faithfully reveals himself and his will to us. As Jesus prayed, "Sanctify them in the truth; thy word is truth" (Jn. 17:17).

David wrote, "Blessed is the man who walks not in the counsel of the wicked, nor stands in the way of sinners, nor sits in the seat of scoffers; but his delight is in the law of the LORD, and on his law he meditates day and night" (Ps. 1:1-2). Did David meditate on the law of God day and night? He had to. He had immense responsibilities for the security of the nation, administration of government, judgment in legal cases and other matters. Out of this he was driven to meditate on the law of God constantly. And what happened? The one who feeds on the law "is like a tree planted by streams of water, that yields its fruit in its season, and its leaf does not wither. In all that he does, he prospers" (v. 3). If a person really wants to know God and God's will for his or her life, the primary means is Bible study.

4. Prayer and worship. Bible study is communication that goes one way. God speaks to us. To round this out, we also need to speak to God. For that we need prayer and worship.

While not necessarily the same thing, worship and prayer are closely related. Prayer is talking to God through praise, confession, thanksgiving or intercession. Worship is meeting with God to praise him, to sing hymns and to expound God's Word. Thus worship will include prayer and meditation. Both prayer and worship are based on our knowledge of

God through Scripture. Worship, if it is to be "in spirit and truth," as Jesus said, must be based upon the truths concerning God which are revealed in the Bible.

Both prayer and worship are essentially a meeting with God and not merely the performance of some religious exercise. Reuben A. Torrey tells of the difficulty he had in the matter of prayer and of how this changed. "The day came when I realized what real prayer meant, realized that prayer was having an audience with God, actually coming into the presence of God and asking and getting things from him. And the realization of that fact transformed my prayer life. Before that, prayer had been a mere duty, and sometimes a very irksome duty, but from that time on, prayer has been not merely a duty but a privilege, one of the most highly esteemed privileges of life. Before that the thought I had was, 'How much time must I spend in prayer?' The thought that now possesses me is, 'How much time may I spend in prayer without neglecting the other privileges and duties of life?' "[6] The same may be said of worship. How much time may I spend in worship and still get on with the other tasks that God has given me?

5. Fellowship. In fellowship we actively express the new relationship with other Christians discussed in chapter nine. Sometimes Christians fall into thinking that because their relationship to God is so personal and wonderful they can do without others. Sometimes they even look down on others as having failed to achieve the high standard of godliness they imagine themselves to possess. They are self-deluded. We should all recognize our need for others and the specific gifts they possess, and be thankful for their fellowship within the company of God's church. When the early Christian community met in Jerusalem, "they devoted themselves to the apostles' teaching and fellowship, to the breaking of bread and the prayers" (Acts 2:42). Fellowship is on a par with other means of grace.

6. Service. If the Christian life is not to be selfish and introverted, there must be service, service to God and to others through evangelism, generosity and other acts of compassion. The book of Acts speaks of this explicitly: "And all who believed were together and had all things in common; and they sold their possessions and goods and distributed them to all, as any had need" (Acts 2:44-45). This does not mean that they all sold everything, still less that all Christians in every place should sell everything. The context speaks of them meeting in "their homes," so some at least retained those. But it does mean that they were generous with their possessions, so concerned were they to meet the needs of others.

Today our service should be in the sharing of our material goods, particularly since we in the West have so many. It should also be in the giving of our time to encourage or teach others, to evangelize or to contribute whatever talent or training we have been given to the growth of Christ's church.

7. The return of Christ. A final source of encouragement and growth in the Christian life is the return of Christ, our "blessed hope" (Tit. 2:13). It is linked to sanctification in 1 John, "Beloved, we are God's children now; it does not yet appear what we shall be, but we know that when he appears we shall be like him, for we shall see him as he is. And every one who thus hopes in him purifies himself as he is pure" (3:2-3).

If we are Christians, we know that God is going to continue his work with us until that day when we are made like Jesus. It may be through death. It may be at Christ's Second Coming. But whenever it is, we know that we will be made like Jesus. We will be pure as he is pure. We will be perfected in love as he is love. We will be virtuous as he is virtuous. John says that if we really believe this, we will try to be as much like him now as possible. This should affect every aspect of our personal lives: prayer, our choices in occupations, in ethics, in use of spare time, even our social concerns. Lord Shaftesbury, the great English social reformer and a mature Christian, said near the end of his life, "I do not think that in the last forty years I have ever lived one conscious hour that was not influenced by the thought of our Lord's return." In this case, the expectation of meeting the Lord face to face was one of the strongest motivations behind his social programs.

How can we purify ourselves? We cannot, but God will do it if we use these means of grace. Robert Herrick, the English poet, once wrote of purification,

Lord, I confess that Thou alone art able
To purify this Augean stable.
Be the seas water and the lands all soap,
Yet if Thy blood not wash me, there's no hope.

Apart from the grace of God there is no hope for anyone. But God has provided the ways for us to grow in grace and in the love and knowledge of our Lord and Savior Jesus Christ.

PART III
THE LIFE OF
THE CHRISTIAN

Then Jesus told his disciples, "If any man would come after me, let him deny himself and take up his cross and follow me." (Mt. 16:24)

For freedom Christ has set us free; stand fast therefore, and do not submit again to a yoke of slavery. (Gal. 5:1)

Do not be conformed to this world but be transformed by the renewal of your mind, that you may prove what is the will of God, what is good and acceptable and perfect. (Rom. 12:2)

Have no anxiety about anything, but in everything by prayer and supplication with thanksgiving let your requests be made known to God. And the peace of God, which passes all understanding, will keep your hearts and your minds in Christ Jesus. (Phil. 4:6-7)

Blessed is the man who walks not in the counsel of the wicked, nor stands in the way of sinners, nor sits in the seat of scoffers; but his delight is in the law of the LORD, and on his law he meditates day and night. (Ps. 1:1-2)

For we are his workmanship, created in Christ Jesus for good works, which God prepared beforehand, that we should walk in them. (Eph. 2:10)

11

EMBRACE THE NEGATIVE

If Madison Avenue executives were trying to attract people to the Christian life, they would stress its positive and fulfilling aspects. They would speak of Christianity as a way to wholeness of life and all happiness. Unfortunately, we who live in the West are so conditioned to this way of thinking (and to precisely this type of Christian evangelism or salesmanship) that we are almost shocked when we learn that the first great principle of Christianity is negative. It is not, as some say, "Come to Christ, and all your troubles will melt away." It is as the Lord himself declared, "If any man would come after me, let him deny himself and take up his cross and follow me. For whoever would save his life will lose it, and whoever loses his life for my sake will find it. For what will it profit a man, if he gains the whole world and forfeits his life?" (Mt. 16:24-26).

If I were writing of Christianity the way our culture writes, I might produce a poem such as this one, found on the wall of a guest room on a Christian college campus:

May the years of your life be pleasant;
  May your beautiful dreams come true,
And in all that you plan and practice
  May blessings descend upon you.

May the trail of your life beat onward
  With many surprises in store,
And the days that are happy with memories
  Prove merely the promise of more.

If we are true to the Word of God, we will speak as Jesus did: "If any one comes to me and does not hate his own father and mother and wife and children and brothers and sisters, yes, and even his own life, he cannot be my disciple. Whoever does not bear his own cross and come after me, cannot be my disciple.... So therefore, whoever of you does not renounce all that he has cannot be my disciple" (Lk. 14:26-27, 33); "Unless a grain of wheat falls into the earth and dies, it remains alone; but if it dies, it bears much fruit. He who loves his life loses it, and he who hates his life in this world will keep it for eternal life" (Jn. 12:24-25); "Blessed are the poor in spirit.... Blessed are those who mourn.... Blessed are the meek.... Blessed are those who are persecuted for righteousness' sake.... Blessed are you when men revile you and persecute you and utter all kinds of evil against you falsely on my account" (Mt. 5:3-5, 10-11).

We recognize that there is a certain amount of Semitic hyperbole in these statements. The One who told us to love each other is not advocating that we cultivate a literal animosity toward the members of our own family. Moreover, this is only one side of the story. Jesus also said, "There is no one who has left house or brothers or sisters or mother or father or children or lands, for my sake and for the gospel, who will not receive a hundredfold now in this time, houses and brothers and sisters and mothers and children and lands, with persecutions, and in the age to come eternal life" (Mk. 10:29-30). But even this is to be *with persecutions,* and it does not eliminate the element of death and denial.

We do not work ourselves up to death and denial, however. Rather, we need them before we can start out at all. Paul shows this by introducing self-sacrifice as the initial principle of the Christian life in his most formal treatment of that life. "I appeal to you therefore, brethren, by the mercies of God, to present your bodies as a living sacrifice, holy and acceptable to God, which is your spiritual worship" (Rom. 12:1).

Calvin understood this theme well. In his comments on Romans 12:1-2, he provides us with some of the most moving appeals in the *Institutes of the Christian Religion:*

If we, then, are not our own [cf. 1 Cor. 6:19] but the Lord's, it is clear what error we must flee, and whither we must direct all the acts of our life. We are not our own: let not our reason nor our will, therefore, sway our plans and deeds. We are not our own: let us therefore not set it as our goal to seek what is expedient for us according to the flesh. We are not our own: in so far as we can, let us therefore forget ourselves and all that is ours.

Conversely, we are God's: let us therefore live for him and die for him. We are God's: let his wisdom and will therefore rule all our actions. We are God's: let all the parts of our life accordingly strive toward him as our only lawful goal [Rom. 14:8; cf. 1 Cor. 6:19]. O, how much has that man profited who, having been taught that he is not his own, has taken away dominion and rule from his own reason that he may yield it to God! For, as consulting our self-interest is the pestilence that most effectively leads to our destruction, so the sole haven of salvation is to be wise in nothing and to will nothing through ourselves but to follow the leading of the Lord alone.[1]

This idea of death in Christ is repeated with slight variations in other places in the Gospels.[2] So it is worthwhile to consider its three parts: (1) we are to deny ourselves, (2) we are to take up Christ's cross and ③ we are to follow Jesus.

Denying Ourselves

Self-denial should not be difficult for any Christian to understand for this is what it means to become a Christian. It means
to have turned your back on any attempt to please God
through your own human abilities and efforts, and instead to
have accepted by faith what God has done in Christ for your
salvation. No one can save himself or herself. So we stop
trying. We die to our efforts. We must say no to them. When
we have done this, we receive God's salvation as a free gift.
So living the Christian life is only a matter of continuing in the
way we have started. This is not difficult to understand, but
it is difficult to apply. This principle is so uncongenial that
even Christians quickly forget it and try to live by other
standards.

It can hardly be otherwise, given our own natural disposi-
tions and the culture in which we live. "We are surrounded
by a world that says No to nothing. When we are surrounded
with this sort of mentality, in which everything is judged by
bigness and by success, then suddenly to be told that in the
Christian life there is to be this strong negative aspect of
saying No to things and No to self, must seem hard. And if it
does not feel hard to us, we are not really letting it speak to
us."[3]

To experience death and denial means we must be willing
to say no and then actually say no to anything that is contrary to God's will for us. This includes *anything contrary to the
Bible.* We are free from law in the sense of being under a
list of rules and regulations. But we are to obey the law in the
sense that it reveals the nature of God and shows us those
areas of life which by the power of God we are to say no to in
order that we might go on with Christ.

The first of the Ten Commandments is an example:
"You shall have no other gods before me." Here is a negative,

an obvious one. It tells us that we are to say no to anything that would take God's rightful place in our lives. Is it an actual idol? We must say no to the idol; we must burn it or destroy it, as many primitive people have done when they have responded to the gospel. Is it money? We must get rid of the money for it is better to be poor and yet close to Christ than rich and far from him. Money is not something that necessarily takes the place of God in a life. It is possible to be a devoted and deeply spiritual Christian and rich at the same time. But if money has become a god, then we must say no to it. Has another person taken the place of God? Has a business? An ambition? Your children? Fame? Achievement? Whatever it is, we must say no to it if it is keeping us from Christ.

If you want to test yourself on this, you may do so with each of the other commandments. "You shall not kill." We are to say no to any desire to take another's life or slander his or her reputation. "You shall not commit adultery." We are to say no to any desire to take another man's wife or another woman's husband. "You shall not steal." We should say no to the desire to take another person's property. If we have not said no at these points, we can hardly pretend that we are living in the newness of Christ's resurrection life. Indeed, we are not living the life of Christ at all.

To experience death and denial we must also say no to anything that is not the will of God for us. This goes beyond the previous point about the law. Not everything permitted in the Word of God is God's will for us. For instance, there is nothing wrong with marriage. In fact, the contrary is true. Marriage has been established by God and has his blessing. Still, marriage may not be the will of God for you; and if it is not, then you must say no to marriage, consciously and deliberately. The same thing holds for a profession, our own conception of ourselves and other things.

Is this hard? Yes, it is hard. It is hard for the strongest saint as well as for the weakest sinner. Here is Augustine's description of the struggle that went on in him:

The new will that had begun in me–and made me want to be free to worship and to enjoy you, God, the only certain joy–was not yet strong enough to overpower the old will that had become tough with age. So there were now two wills battling it out inside me, one old, one new; one carnal, one spiritual; and in the conflict they ripped my soul to pieces.

From my own experience I know, therefore, what Paul meant when he said, "The flesh lusts against the Spirit, and the Spirit against the flesh." I was on both sides, but mostly I was on the side that I approved in myself, rather than the side I disapproved. When I did things that I knew were wrong I did not act willingly, but just endured them; but habit had been reinforced by that part of my will that had deserted to the enemy, so it was by my own will that I found myself in a spot I didn't want to be in. And what point is there in complaining when a sinner gets what is coming to him? I used to excuse myself by saying I had no clear concept of truth, and that was why I still followed the ways of the world rather than serve you. Now, however, I was quite certain about the truth; and still I kept myself grounded and refused to enlist in your service. I was more afraid of getting rid of my frustrations than I was of being frustrated.

Thus I was put under pressure by the oppressions of the world, but I took it all with a light heart, like a man sound asleep. When I did think about you, my meditations were like the feeble struggles of a man who is trying to wake up but is overcome with drowsiness and falls back to sleep. I had no answer when you said, "Awake, O sleeper, and arise from the dead, and Christ shall give you light." You used every possible means to communicate to me the truth of your words. You had me under conviction so that I could give no reply except a lazy and drowsy, "Yes, Lord, yes, I'll get to it right away, just don't bother me for a little while." But "right away" didn't happen right away; and "a little while" turned out to be a very long while. In my inmost self I delighted in the law of God, but I perceived that there was in my bodily members a different law

fighting against the law that my reason approved and making me a
prisoner under the law that was in my members, the law of sin. For
the law of sin is the force of habit, by which the mind is carried along
and held prisoner against its will, deservedly, of course, because
it slid into the habit by its own choice. Messed-up creature that I
was, who was there to rescue this doomed body? God alone through
Jesus Christ our Lord! [4]

Augustine's words are a classic statement of the <u>divided</u> <u>will</u>
and of the difficulty of surrendering that will to God. On the
other hand, here is a classic statement of the blessing of having
denied oneself for Christ—from the _Imitation of Christ_ by
Thomas à Kempis: "O Lord, thou knowest what is the better
way; let this or that be done as thou shalt please. Give what
thou wilt, and how much thou wilt, and when thou wilt. Do
with me as thou knowest, and as best pleaseth thee, and is most
for thy honor. Set me where thou wilt, and deal with me in all
things just as thou wilt. . . . When could it be ill with me, when
thou wert present? I had rather be poor for thee, than rich
without thee. I rather choose to be a pilgrim on earth with
thee, than without thee to possess heaven. Where thou art,
there is heaven; and where thou art not, there is death and
hell."[5]

How can you know when you have said no? When you have
stopped complaining. If you are murmuring, as the Israelites
murmured in the wilderness, you have not really turned your
back on Egypt. If you have stopped murmuring, you are
ready to press on.

Taking Up Christ's Cross

The second expression of the principle of death and denial is
death itself, which Jesus points to by saying that we are to take
up our cross in his service. To understand this image we must
first leave behind the meaning usually given to it. Today when
people speak of bearing their cross or taking up their cross,
what they usually have in mind is stoic endurance of some in-

escapable hardship: sickness, an alcoholic spouse, blindness, an uncongenial place of work or similar limitations. This is not what Christ meant. In Jesus' day the cross was a symbol of death, a means of execution. So Jesus really referred to our dying, dying to self—a step beyond mere self-denial. Moreover, in saying that we were to "take up" our cross, he was indicating that our act is to be a voluntary and continuous activity.

Taking up our cross is beyond mere self-denial because it is possible to deny ourselves many things and yet not utterly give ourselves. It is possible to stop somewhere between the indecision of Augustine and that total surrender we find in à Kempis. We often do what Jacob did (in Gen. 32) when he was returning to the land of promise after twenty years of working for his uncle Laban. Jacob had cheated his brother and had to run away and live with his uncle Laban on the other side of the desert. His brother had said he was going to kill him, and he was afraid then. But twenty years had passed, and he had forgotten the force of the threat.

Yet as Jacob got closer and closer to the land from which he had fled and in which Esau was still living, he became frightened again. He began to remember what he had done. He began to remember the threats Esau had made. Every step he took became more and more difficult. Finally, he came to the brook Jabbok and looked across to where he knew Esau lived. I believe that if he could have gone back, he would have. But things were so difficult with Laban that Laban had said in effect, "If you come back, it's a fight to the death." Retreat was cut off. Jacob had nowhere to go but forward. Finally he said to his servants, "Let's take the lay of the land. You go over first and find out what Esau is doing."

The servants went. But they had not gone very far when they met Esau coming with a band of four hundred men. This was an army. So the servants went back and said to Jacob, "Your brother knows you're coming, all right. He's coming to

meet you. The only difficulty is that he has his army with him."
Now Jacob was truly afraid. What was he to do? Resourcefully
he looked around at his possessions and decided that he
would begin to give them up. He would first give the things
he did not care too much about.

First he took a flock of two hundred goats. He sent them
over the Jabbok with his servants. He said to the servants,
"When Esau sees you and asks, 'Whose servants are you? And
where are you going? And who owns these animals?' you must
say, 'They belong to your servant Jacob; they are a present
sent to my lord, Esau; and Jacob himself is behind us.' "
Jacob thought this would soften him up.

But he thought, "Suppose Esau isn't satisfied with the
goats? I'd better send some ewes." And so he sent two hundred of them. Then he sent thirty camels, followed by forty
cows, followed by ten bulls, followed by twenty female don-
keys and ten foals. As you read about it in Genesis it is hilar-
ious. All Jacob's possessions were stretched out in bands across
the country going toward Esau. In every case the servants
were to say, "These are a present for my lord, Esau."

Finally, all the possessions were gone. Jacob did not have
any more camels or sheep or goats or bulls or cows to give up.
But he still had his wives and children. So he said, "I'd better
give them up too." He took Leah, who was the least favorite
wife, and he sent her first with her children. Then he took
Rachel, who was the favorite wife, and he sent her with her
children. And there at last, all alone and trembling, was Jacob.
He still had not given himself.

That is what we do. God gets close to us, and we are a little
afraid of him. So we say, "I'll placate him; I'll give him my
money." But God does not seem to be satisfied with that, and
we do not quite understand why. We say, "I'll give him my
time. I'll serve on the church board. I'll teach a Sunday-school
class." At last we give him our family. But we do not give ourselves. And the time comes when we are standing all alone,

naked in his sight and God sends his angel to wrestle us to the point of personal submission.

The only trouble with this illustration is that it suggests that achieving death to self is a once-for-all surrender when actually it is the continuous business of daily obedience and discipline. There can be moments of important personal crisis and decision; there probably have to be. But the battle is not won even then, for these decisions must be followed by continuous daily decisions to say no to ourselves in order to say yes to God. The Greek text indicates this by the use of the present (continuative) sense: "Let him take up his cross (repeatedly and continuously) and keep on following me."

Daily Discipleship

This leads to the next point: discipleship. For when Jesus said that we are to deny ourselves and take up our cross he obviously did not mean that we are literally to die or to cease to function. We are to enter by that gate into a path of lifelong discipleship. In that discipleship the principles with which we started out, self-denial and death to self, are determinative.

How do we learn such denial, such death to our own plans and interests? There is only one way. We must follow Jesus and constantly keep our eyes on him. He is the supreme example of self-denial. He said no even to the glories of heaven in order to become man and die for our salvation (Phil. 2: 5-11). The author of Hebrews captures this solution when, in the verses immediately following his great chapter on the heroes of the faith, he writes, "Therefore, since we are surrounded by so great a cloud of witnesses, let us also lay aside every weight, and sin which clings so closely, and let us run with perseverance the race that is set before us, looking to Jesus the pioneer and perfecter of our faith, who for the joy that was set before him endured the cross, despising the shame, and is seated at the right hand of the throne of God" (Heb. 12:1-2).

Jesus taught this also. We notice when we study the verses on death and denial carefully that in nearly every case they are set in the context of Jesus' teaching concerning his own suffering and death by crucifixion. Mark ten is the clearest example. In that chapter Jesus is teaching about discipleship showing that his disciples must all be bound by the revealed Word of God (vv. 1-12), that they must come to God with the simple faith of children (vv. 13-16) and that possessions are often a hindrance and deterrent to discipleship (vv. 17-31). In this last section he introduces the matter of loss of family and lands for his sake and for the gospel.

Then we read, "And they were on the road, going up to Jerusalem, and Jesus was walking ahead of them; and they were amazed, and those who followed were afraid. And taking the twelve again, he began to tell them what was to happen to him, saying, 'Behold, we are going up to Jerusalem; and the Son of man will be delivered to the chief priests and the scribes, and they will condemn him to death, and deliver him to the Gentiles; and they will mock him, and spit upon him, and scourge him, and kill him; and after three days he will rise' " (Mk. 10:32-34).

Jesus was asking the fullest possible measure of devotion from those who followed him. They were to give up everything. But he was not asking them to do something he was not willing to do himself. He was providing them with a perfect example.

He also spoke of his resurrection and thus taught that the way of denial and death, though it involves a true and sometimes painful death to our own desires, is nevertheless the way to the fullness of living. Paul writes in Romans, "If we have been united with him in a death like his, we shall certainly be united with him in a resurrection like his" (Rom. 6:5). It is the same in Galatians. "I have been crucified with Christ; it is no longer I who live, but Christ who lives in me; and the life I now live in the flesh I live by faith in the Son of God, who loved me and gave himself for me" (Gal. 2:20). In the biblical scheme of things death is always followed by life, crucifixion by resurrection. It is this that is truly exciting and for which we are willing to die.

When we give up trying to run our own life or when we give up what seems so precious and so utterly indispensable to us, it is then (and only then) that we suddenly find the true joy of being a Christian and enter into a life so freed from obsession that we can hardly understand how it could have had such a hold on us.

This is the primary difference between a joyless and a joyful Christian, a defeated and a victorious one. Death and resurrection! Joyless Christians may have died and risen with Christ in some abstract sense, so they can in the same sense be termed new creatures in Christ. But they have certainly never known it in practice. Joyful Christians have found satisfaction in whatever God gives them and are truly satisfied. They have said no to anything that might keep them from the richness of God's own blessing and presence and have risen to new life.

12 FREEDOM, FREEDOM

In the last chapter we saw the seeming paradox at the heart of the Christian life: we must die to self in order to live to God. There is another as well: we must become Christ's slave before we can be truly free. These are only apparent paradoxes, however. In the ultimate sense there are no paradoxes in Scripture. The doctrine of the Trinity might be thought to be a paradox, but it is not really. When we say that God is both a Trinity and a unity, we mean only that he is three in one sense and one in another. When we speak of the paradox between election and free will or between free will and the bondage of the will, we mean that the will is free in some areas (the least important) and bound in others (the most important). Similarly, when we speak of Christians being slaves to Christ and yet free, we mean that they become servants in one sense so they can become all that God intends them to be.

Christian freedom is like that of a man or woman in marriage. In one sense they are bound to each other; they are not free to love and relate to others in the way that they are obliged to love and relate to their spouse. But in another sense they really are free. They are free to be themselves within the marriage, acting as what they really are—a married man and woman. They are free from the fear of rejection because of their mutual commitment. They are even free to love others with a love that complements their love in marriage.

Pursuit of Freedom

The key to discovering freedom is to be what one has been created to be—an obedient and grateful servant of the Most High. The difficulty for many people is that they wish to be what they are not or can never be; thus, they are doomed to a life of frustration. Freedom has been defined as "the ability to fulfill one's destiny, to function in terms of one's ultimate goal."[1] In modern culture freedom has more often been conceived as autonomy. But because this is a universe created and maintained by a sovereign God, no creature is or can be autonomous.

The pursuit of wealth is one attempt to achieve freedom apart from God or even from God himself. It is probably the dominant goal of most in the West and increasingly of the rest of the world as well. If asked, most who pursue this goal would deny that their interest is in money itself. "We are not materialists," they would say. "Money is freedom. Our pursuit of affluence is merely that we might have liberty to go where we wish and do what we want. We do not want to be tied to a particular job or place because of inadequate finances."

Christians have no quarrel with anyone striving to attain a good standard of living. Poverty has truely binding effects in life. But it is not true that money is freedom. Freedom is a matter of the soul or mind. At best affluence deals only with the lifestyle or mobility of people. At times the wealthy are even imprisoned by their wealth, as some testify. Others are afraid of theft and barricade themselves as a protection against it.

/ *Refusal to make commitments* is a second way some try to find freedom apart from God. Some couples live together without being married because they "want to be free," meaning they want the option of ending the relationship if they grow tired of it. A bumper sticker proclaims, "Happiness is being single." In job interviews many will not promise a prospective employer to remain with the company for more than a test period because they "want to be free to move on."

But the flaw is that freedom is only freedom if you use it. To make no commitments is really to do (or be) nothing at all. A commitment to many things or persons actually *brings* freedom. In Christianity a commitment to Christ brings freedom from sin, alienation, guilt, aimlessness and eventually death through the resurrection. True, Christians are not free to sin, but they are free to serve. They are not free to hate, but they are set free to love. They are free to follow the path God sets before them.

/ *A rejection of the past* is another false attempt to find freedom. Not only are yesterday's standards of morality rejected, but even yesterday's standards for doing anything. Anything new is better than anything old simply because it is new. This view is based on an unwillingness to be bound by anything others may have done or required, particularly in the realm of ethics.

Yet the law does not go away simply because we reject it, nor is conscience so easily shouted down. This might be possible were we our own makers and therefore truly autonomous, being responsible to no one but ourselves. But we are not our own creators. We are not autonomous. And we are responsible to many: parents, employers, spiritual leaders, the state, God. What is needed is not a rejection of the past and its standards but rather a freedom of mind and purpose which enables us to choose from the past, retaining what is best and adding to it on the basis of right conduct both before God and others.

/ *Rejection of all authority* is the last of the major contemporary attempts to achieve freedom apart from God. Ultimately, this is the rejection of God, for the various human authorities that we know come from him (Rom. 13:1-2). What takes their place? The individual. We each become our own authority. Friedrich Wilhelm Nietzsche, the philosopher, held out for the absolute autonomy of the individual, but his own later insanity is a testimony to the futility of this determination.

Any attempt to establish freedom apart from the presuppositions of Christianity is doomed because it makes freedom hang on the individual's own ability, which is not enough to sustain it. Reinhold Niebuhr analyzes this failure in an essay on "Individuality in Modern Culture."[2] He traces the destruction of individual freedom (which, he maintains, has been given to the world by Christianity) through three philosophies: naturalism, idealism and romanticism. Naturalism failed to maintain individual freedom because it reduced humans to machines. Idealism failed because, although it stressed the higher, spiritual or rational capacities of the individual, it found these only in a universal Self or Spirit in which the individual is lost. In romanticism the self became everything, but in the end all except a few like Nietzsche were forced to recoil from the pretensions of this individual self-glorification.

Niebuhr sums up these abortive attempts to establish freedom without the presuppositions of Christianity:

The simple fact is that both the obviously partial and unique and the supposedly universal values of history can be both appreciated and judged only in terms of a religious faith which has discovered the centre and source of life to be beyond and yet within historical existence. This is the God who is both Creator and Judge revealed in Biblical faith. . . . Without the presuppositions of the Christian faith the individual is either nothing or becomes everything. In the Christian faith man's insignificance as a creature, involved in the process of nature and time, is lifted into significance by the mercy and power of God in which his life is sustained. But his significance _as a free spirit is understood as subordinate to the freedom of God. His inclination to abuse his freedom, to overestimate his power and significance and to become everything is understood as the primal sin. It is because man is inevitably involved in this primal sin that he is bound to meet God first of all as a judge, who humbles his pride and brings his vain imagination to naught._"[3]

Three Freedoms

What does God say about freedom? Apart from the grace of God in Jesus Christ we are not free. Jesus himself said, "Every one who commits sin is a slave to sin" (Jn. 8:34). Freedom is found in obeying the laws of God, but we know that we disobey those laws. In fact, we have lost our ability to obey and so have lost our ability to be free. "Ever since Adam and Eve fell in paradise, the whole of mankind by natural generation is encompassed in a terrible rebellion, corruption, and slavery in which, even in spite of some desires that we may have from time to time to do what is right, we are constantly carried along. So we sigh deeply in our heart, 'What a wretched man I am! Who will rescue me?' (Rom. 7:24). 'How shall I get that emancipation? How shall I get freedom?' We say, 'Give me liberty, because I am already encompassed in death.' "[4] The gospel of God's grace in Jesus Christ says that we can be free to fulfill that destiny for which God has created us.

First, the gospel provides us with freedom from condemnation by God's law and thus _freedom of conscience._[5] Freedom must begin here. Other freedoms will be shallow unless we are liberated from this condemnation. We gain this freedom through faith in Jesus Christ who died in our place taking our condemnation on himself. When we look to ourselves we must admit as does the 1848 Confession of the Evangelical Free Church of Geneva, Switzerland: "All men are born sinners, unable to do good before God, inclined to evil, bringing condemnation and death on themselves by a just judgment" (Article IV). But when we look to Christ we find one who has freed us from that condemnation by dying for our sins. He has paid the full penalty required by the law for our transgressions and has given us a standing before God which is the same as if we had never sinned at all.

The law of God is now no longer a threat to us. It is true that we have disobeyed it, but it has been dealt with. We now stand before the almighty God with clean records and liberated consciences.

It was this freedom that impressed the apostle Paul so deeply. He had given himself to obedience to the law. But the law was a stern taskmaster, and he had been burdened by it. He may have claimed to have kept the law perfectly, according to human interpretations (Phil. 3:6). But he still was not righteous as God counts righteousness, and he sensed it (Acts 26: 14). What was he to do? Through the gospel of Christ he discovered a righteousness apart from the law, which met the requirements of God perfectly. At this point he cried, "There is therefore now no condemnation for those who are in Christ Jesus. For the law of the Spirit of life in Christ Jesus has set me free from the law of sin and death. For God has done what the law, weakened by the flesh, could not do: sending his own Son in the likeness of sinful flesh and for sin, he condemned sin in the flesh, in order that the just requirement of the law might be fulfilled in us, who walk not according to the flesh but according to the Spirit" (Rom. 8:1-4).

Similarly, in Galatians, after a spirited defense of justification by faith alone, Paul rhapsodizes, "For freedom Christ has set us free; stand fast therefore, and do not submit again to a yoke of slavery" (Gal. 5:1).

Each of these passages leads immediately to *freedom of obedience.* Each is part of an argument dealing, not merely with freedom from the law's condemnation, but also with a very practical freedom. The Romans passage comes immediately after a chapter detailing Paul's personal struggle between the desires of his new nature and the sinful desires of his old nature. The passage in Galatians leads into a discussion of the life of the Spirit which is a result of justification. Being freed from the condemnation of the law and being given a new nature, believers are now set free from their old desires and rebellion and can obey God.

Once Jesus had been speaking to the Jews of his day about the source and nature of his teachings, and many had believed on him in a rudimentary sense. But recognizing this, Jesus encouraged them to stay with him and continue to learn from him. He said, "If you continue in my word, you are truly my disciples, and you will know the truth, and the truth will make you free."

This infuriated some who were there, perhaps some unbelievers though the text does not say so explicitly. They replied, "We are descendants of Abraham, and have never been in bondage to any one. How is it that you say, 'You will be made free'?" This was ridiculous, of course. For years the Jews had been slaves in Egypt. During the period of the Judges there were at least seven occasions when the nation came under the domination of foreigners. There was the seventy-year Babylonian captivity. Even as they were talking to Jesus they were watched over by Roman soldiers and carried coins in their purses that showed Rome's rule over Palestine. This very fact made them quite sensitive to the issue of freedom.

But Jesus did not try to show how deluded they were in their thoughts about political freedom. Instead, he answered, "Truly, truly, I say to you, every one who commits sin is a slave to sin. . . . If the Son makes you free, you will be free indeed" (Jn. 8:34-36).

Freedom comes from the new nature of Christ within. Consequently, desiring now to please God we do what pleases him, not because we are forced to do so by the strictures of the law but simply because we desire to please God. Is the law of no value then? On the contrary, it is of great value. It shows us what pleases God.

This is particularly important in questionable matters. What may I do on Sunday? What occupations are open to me as a Christian? May I smoke? Drink? Play cards? Go to movies? In some of these cases there are obvious limits placed on our conduct. But the Bible does not answer all such questions specifically; and if we are trying to find an answer in this way, we will only be bound up by it and lose the freedom we should have.

Calvin put it well.

When consciences once ensnare themselves, they enter a long and inextricable maze, not easy to get out of. If a man begins to doubt whether he may use linen for sheets, shirts, handkerchiefs and napkins, he will afterward be uncertain also about hemp; finally, doubt will even arise over tow. For he will turn over in his mind whether he can sup without napkins, or go without a handkerchief. If any man should consider daintier food unlawful, in the end he will not be at peace before God, when he eats either black bread or common victuals, while it occurs to him that he could sustain his body on even coarser foods. If he boggles at sweet wine, he will not with clear conscience drink even flat wine, and finally he will come to the point of considering it wrong to step upon a straw across his path, as the saying goes. [6]

The third area of Christian freedom is linked to the other two: *freedom of knowledge.* Through knowledge of who we are as sinners, and of who God is and what he has done in Christ for our salvation, we are saved from the law's condemnation and launched on the Christian life. Having come to know God as he is revealed in Christ, we find that we want to go on learning about him. We also find ourselves growing in the genuine freedom which knowledge of God brings. "You will know the truth, and the truth will make you free."

If Henry has no education, the professions are closed to him. He can do manual work, but not white-collar work. If Sharon is illiterate, even more doors are closed. She will have difficulty finding anything other than menial forms of employment. The fullest enjoyment of the arts—music, drama, sculpture—will probably be excluded for her as well. Likewise, those who do not know the teachings of the Word of God cannot thrive spiritually. They will be bound by misconceptions of God's nature, superstition and the prejudices of others. Only those who are increasingly coming to know and love God's Word can grow in freedom.

Once some Christians in Hong Kong talked with an eighty-two-year-old woman who had shortly before been released from China. She was a Christian, but her vocabulary was filled with much of the terminology of communism.

"When you were back in China, were you free to gather together with other Christians to worship?" they asked her.

"Oh, no," she answered. "Since the liberation no one is permitted to gather together for Christian services."

"But surely you were able to get together in small groups and discuss the Christian faith?"

"No, we are not," was the woman's reply. "Since the liberation all such meetings are forbidden."

"Were you free to read your Bible?"

"Since the liberation no one is free to read the Bible."

Freedom does not consist in the words _liberation_ or _freedom_ alone, but in the reality which Christianity brings.

13 KNOWING THE WILL OF GOD

There are not many questions that Christians ask more often than, "What is God's plan for my life? How can I know it? And how can I be sure that I know it?" These questions come naturally to Christian people. But even if they did not, they would be forced upon us by the Bible's teaching that God wants us to know his will and embrace it gratefully. This is the implication of Romans 12:1-2, verses that we have looked at several times already in other contexts: "I appeal to you therefore, brethren, by the mercies of God, to present your bodies as a living sacrifice, holy and acceptable to God, which is your spiritual worship. Do not be conformed to this world but be transformed by the renewal of your mind, that you may prove what is the will of God, what is good and acceptable and perfect." We are to deny ourselves and mature in Christian character by means of an inward transformation so we can understand the perfect will of God for our lives.

In Philippians, after Paul has spoken of the goal of the Christian life and of his own desire to press on toward it, he

154 Awakening to God

also writes, "Let those of us who are mature be thus minded; and if in anything you are otherwise minded, God will reveal that also to you" (3:15).

The Psalms are filled with this theme, particularly those of David who possessed a strong sense of need for God's guidance. In Psalm 25 he asks, "Make me to know thy ways, O LORD; teach me thy paths. Lead me in thy truth, and teach me" (vv. 4-5). Then he declares, "Good and upright is the LORD; therefore he instructs sinners in the way. He leads the humble in what is right, and teaches the humble his way" (vv. 8-9). Psalm 16:7 declares, "I bless the LORD who gives me counsel." A psalm of Asaph says, "I am continually with thee; thou dost hold my right hand. Thou dost guide me with thy counsel" (Ps. 73:23-24).

These verses do not mean that we will always be able to see more than one step ahead in the Christian life. They do not even mean that we shall be able always to see ahead at all. But they do mean that God has a plan for us and that he promises to lead us in it, revealing the steps that are necessary for us to know as we go forward.

The Wills of God

I need to clarify something before we go on. When we speak of knowing the will of God we commonly think of that which God does not promise to reveal and usually does not reveal. God does not reveal his secret or hidden purposes (Deut. 29: 29). What he does reveal is that kind of life or character which pleases him.

Thus we see already that there are different meanings attached to the word *will*. In the Bible, one is that of the *sovereign* or *efficacious* will of God. This will is beyond anything we can fully know on earth. Indeed, it provides the origin of all things and orders them. God's will is absolute. It is unlimited. It is determined only by God himself. God does not need to consult anyone in formulating his plans, and he does not need help from anyone in carrying them out. God's will is independent. It is fixed. It does not need to adapt to changing circumstances. It is omnipotent. This is the sense in John 6:40, in which Jesus says, "This is the will of my Father, that every one who sees the Son and believes in him should have eternal life."

Another meaning of _will_ in Scripture is the _disposition_ of God or what pleases him. In the Lord's Prayer is the petition which says, "Thy will be done." This does not refer to the sovereign or efficacious will of God, for if that were the case, there would be no need to pray for it. God's will in that sense will be done whether we like it or not. In the Lord's Prayer the request is rather that what pleases God might be increasingly realized in our lives and in the lives of others.

So when we speak of wanting to know God's will, are we asking to know God's hidden councils, those which are the expression of his sovereign will, or are we seeking to know what pleases him? If it is the former, we are doomed to frustration. We will not learn God's hidden councils for the simple reason that they are hidden. If we are seeking to know what pleases God, much can be said, for God has revealed that to us. "God wills our righteousness. God wills our obedience. And the law of God clearly reflects something of his will in the perceptive sense, the sense of his disposition."[1]

Our Will and God's

But how do I know what pleases God in the specific circumstances of my life? How do I know whether I should go into an academic or business career? Whom should I marry? What church should I join? How should I spend my time? For work? For Christian activities? For recreation and relaxation? In what ways shall I spend the money that I earn? There are countless similar questions that confront us, and while some of these may concern God's hidden purposes, not all of them do. Barring supernatural disclosures of God's will, which God sometimes gives but does not encourage us to count on, there are three principles which we are to follow.

The first is a precondition which can often solve a problem instantly: *we must be willing to do the will of God even before we know what it is.* John 7:17 states clearly, "If any man's will is to do his will, he shall know whether the teaching is from God or whether I am speaking on my own authority." Jesus is referring to the truth or falsity of his doctrine which had been challenged by the Jewish leaders. But in answering this he taught the broader principle that knowing the will of God consists largely in being willing to do it. The difficulty with most of us is that, in spite of what we profess, we actually most want to do what we want to do—and in seeking guidance we are actually hoping that God will come around to our way of thinking.

Richard was a prominent leader in church. He was deeply concerned about his line of work. He felt secure in doing what he was doing, but he was uncertain about the location. He felt he should work in another state. Unfortunately, he had no job offers from that state though he had been praying for this. On one occasion he prayed very specifically. He got down beside his desk, on his knees, and spoke to God along these lines: "Dear God, I am so uncertain about this thing. I do not know what to do. What I really need is a sign from you. I need somebody from the state I am interested in to call me up and offer me a position." While he was still on his knees the phone beside him rang. It was long distance, and the person on the other end offered him a job in precisely the area of the country he had been praying about. But he did not accept the position. He stayed where he was and to this day says, "Perhaps I should have said yes when that telephone rang."

I am not quite ready to say that my friend should have taken the new job. Perhaps he should have. But this may have been God's way of showing him that his basic problem in knowing the will of God was that he did not really want to do it, regardless of what he was praying or what answers he received. In most cases, our difficulties with knowing the will of God are in this area.

When I counsel others on knowing God's will, similar problems often arise. After we have talked and I have led them to consider relevant passages of Scripture, they raise objections. Either the verses do not apply to their situation, they are unreasonable, they cannot be obeyed, or some such thing. This usually tells me that the difficulty is not in knowing what God desires but in wanting to do it.

How are we to become willing to do God's will? We must first recognize our unwillingness. Then, we must submit to those Christian disciplines by which we are "transformed" from within by the renewal of our minds that we might "prove what is the will of God" (Rom. 12:2). Prayer is one of these disciplines. It is by prayer that we stop in the rush of our daily routine, think about God and his ways, review our lives in that light and then ask God's forgiveness for past failures and his guidance for the future. Christian fellowship is another discipline. We need the support, interest and loving correction of others. Most important is a regular program of Bible study, which leads us to the second important principle for knowing God's will.

This second principle is substantive: *God has revealed his will in Scripture.* God's hidden will—involving elements of our future lives and occupations—is not revealed anywhere, even in Scripture. So we do not approach the Bible in a magical way to see whether we should marry John or Bill or Mary or Carol. But what God desires is made abundantly clear in Scripture.

The Bible limits our options. It may not tell us whether we are to marry Bill or Carol, but it does tell us that we are not to live with either one before we are married. It condemns fornication. Similarly, it may not tell us whether we are to be a doctor or a lawyer, but it tells us that we are not to be a thief or a prostitute or enter any line of work which may damage others.

The Bible also gives us guidelines on which we may operate. One is stated in the verses we have referred to twice earlier: Romans 12:1-2. It tells us that God wills our sanctification. Anything that contributes to our growth in holiness is an aspect of God's will for us. Anything that hinders that growth is not his will. Above everything, God is interested in having us become like Jesus Christ. "For this is the will of God, your sanctification" (1 Thess. 4:3).

Colossians 3:23 is an expression of God's will for our work. "Whatever your task, work heartily, as serving the Lord and not men." This principle applies particularly to students or to those just starting out in a career. A member of my congregation once remarked that all too often young Christians interpret a difficulty in their work or schooling as an indication that what they are doing is not God's will for them when, actually, it is probably God's indication that they should work harder at it. This verse tells us that God wants us to do well in everything we are given to do.

A guideline that is closely related to this is found in Ephesians 6:5-6: "Slaves, be obedient to those who are your earthly masters, with fear and trembling, in singleness of heart, as to Christ; not in the way of eyeservice, as men-pleasers, but as servants of Christ, doing the will of God from the heart." This guideline is especially for those who have a difficult boss or a difficult teacher. The Bible says it is God's will that you should avoid gossiping about him or her and instead work as well as you are able. You should do it not only when the boss is watching but also when he or she is not watching—as unto the Lord and not unto men.

Other verses tell us that we are to make a sober analysis of our gifts to see where we might be most useful, and also to seek the guidance of our brothers and sisters in the church. The church is often the one that gives a call for a vocation (see Acts 13:1-3).

Doubtful Situations

But we must admit that there are situations where matters are not so clear. Can I work for a company that produces war materials? Can I drink alcoholic beverages? Can I enter politics? The theater?

To answer these questions we begin with grace. Romans 6:14 states, "Sin will have no dominion over you, since you are not under law but under grace." This verse is set in a context of godly living. The way to godliness, then, will never be found by organizing a body of Christians to declare whether or not movies, alcohol, cards, the Masons, going to war or whatever is proper. "You are not under law but under grace."

Does being free of law mean that we are at liberty to do as we please? Should we sin that grace may abound? On the contrary, "Now that you have been set free from sin and have become slaves of God, the return you get is sanctification and its end, eternal life" (Rom. 6:22). Living by grace actually leads to holiness, for our desire is to please the one who has saved us by that grace.

To determine God's will in doubtful matters we should next realize that although all things are permissible for Christians—because we are not under law but under grace—still all things are not helpful. This is true first because the thing may gain a harmful control over us. " 'All things are lawful for me,' but not all things are helpful. 'All things are lawful for me,' but I will not be enslaved by anything" (1 Cor. 6:12). Paul knew that God had not set him free from sin simply to be captured by mere things.

The question to ask is, "Am I using things or are things using me?" Take food, the first of Paul's examples (1 Cor. 6: 13-14). Nothing can be as obviously good for a person as food; it is necessary for bodily strength as well as mental health. But it is possible for a person to become so addicted to overeating that the good end is thwarted and the person's health endangered. Hence, certain eating habits should be avoided. The second of Paul's examples is sex (1 Cor. 7:5-20). This, too, is good. It is a gift from God. Within the bonds of marriage it is a force for strength in the home as well as an expression of close union. But it too can be destructive. It can control the person instead of the person controlling it. In this form sex can destroy the very values it was created to maintain. The Bible teaches that Christians must never use things—food, sex, drugs, alcohol, cars, homes, stocks or whatever—in such a way that we actually fall under their power. In some of these cases, 1 Corinthians 6:12 is an unequivocal warning to avoid them.

Later on in 1 Corinthians Paul gives a second reason why all things are not helpful: the freedom of one believer may hurt the spiritual growth of another. " 'All things are lawful,' but not all things are helpful. 'All things are lawful,' but not all things build up" (1 Cor. 10:23). The verses that follow show that he is thinking of the well-being and growth of fellow Christians.

Taking this verse to its extreme would mean to derive your standards of conduct entirely from what other Christians say or think. If you do that, you are either going to become hypocritical, schizophrenic or mad. But the verse does mean that there are going to be situations in which you will have to avoid certain things even though they are right in themselves because you won't want to harm others. Suppose you have been witnessing to Sharon, a friend of yours. She has been having a hard time overcoming a disposition to sexual sins. She has become a Christian. Still the lure of the flesh is with her. This verse means that you had better not take her to see X-rated movies. What is more, you had best not go yourself, for she may be harmed by your freedom. In the same way, you are not to serve alcohol to Christians for whom it is a serious problem; for their sake, if necessary, you are to avoid it also.

Moreover, we should be consistent in our abstinence over a long period of time so as not to appear two-faced or hypocritical. Paul wrote, "Therefore, if food is a cause of my brother's falling, I will never eat meat, lest I cause my brother to fall" (1 Cor. 8:13). Never! And this from the same apostle who defended the cause of Christian liberty from law sucessfully before the Jerusalem apostles (Acts 15:1-29; Gal. 2: 1-10). Clearly, it will sometimes be costly if we are to watch the effect our conduct may have on other Christians.

Lastly, in deciding how to handle doubtful matters we should seek to choose the best. It is stated well in Philippians 4:8. "Finally, brethren, whatever is true, whatever is honorable, whatever is just, whatever is pure, whatever is lovely, whatever is gracious, if there is any excellence, if there is anything worthy of praise, think about these things."

This does not exclude the best things in our society, whether explicitly Christian or not. The heart of the verse lies in the fact (not always noticed by commentators and Bible teachers) that the virtues mentioned here are pagan virtues. These words do not occur in the great lists of Christian virtues which include love, joy, peace, long-suffering and so on. On the whole they are taken from the writings of Greek philosophers and moralists. In using these words Paul is actually sanctifying, as it were, the generally accepted virtues of pagan morality. He is saying that although the pursuit of the best by Christians will obviously include spiritual things, it will not mean the exclusion of the best values that the world has to offer. The things that are acknowledged to be honorable by the best people everywhere are also worthy to be cultivated by Christians. Consequently Christians can love all that is true, honest, just, pure, lovely and of good report, wherever we find it. We can rejoice in the best of art and good literature. We can thrill to great music. We can thrive on beautiful architecture. We can also thank God for giving people, even in their fallen state, the ability to create such beauty.

Take confidence from the promise of God's presence that accompanies Paul's words. He often wrote parenthetically in his letters, and he does so here. The result is that the first half of verse 9 partially distorts the meaning of the sentence. The first half says, "What you have learned and received and heard and seen in me, do." As the verse stands you would tend to think that the promise of God's presence is attached to it. Actually, as the Greek syntax, which repeats the word "whatever" throughout verse 8 and into verse 9, makes clear, it is attached to verse 8, and the promise is: "Whatever is true, honorable, just, pure, and lovely, think on these things . . . and the God of peace will be with you." When you pursue the highest things in life, both spiritually and secularly, then the God of peace will be with you. You shall have the confidence that he will bless and guide as you seek to please him.

Looking to Jesus

This brings us to the third of the three principles mentioned earlier in this chapter. The first principle was that we must be willing to do the will of God even before we know what it is; the second, that we must get our guidelines from Scripture. The third is the principle of *daily and even hourly fellowship with the Lord.* Psalm 32:8 states it by saying, "I will instruct you and teach you the way you should go; I will counsel you with my eye." If the Lord is to guide us with *his* eye, he must first catch *our* eye. And this means that we must look to him regularly throughout the day.[2]

Of course, this is what we really need and desire—fellowship with one who knows what we should do and how we should do it. We need more than a mere instruction manual. John White says, "You may seek guidance, but God desires to give something better: Himself."[3] What God has really provided is a Guide. We are to stay close to him and follow his leading.

14 TALKING TO GOD

Through Bible study God speaks to us. By prayer we speak to God. Both are as necessary in developing a personal relationship as genuine two-way conversation.

But prayer is even more than conversation. It is a privilege. We place ourselves in the will of God as best we know how. Then, as children approaching our mother or father, we request what we need, knowing that we shall receive it. Prayer is our response to Christ's promise: "Whatever you ask in my name, I will do it, that the Father may be glorified in the Son; if you ask anything in my name, I will do it" (Jn. 14:13-14).

Reuben A. Torrey, in one of his books on prayer, has listed eleven reasons why prayer is important: (1) because there is a devil and because prayer is the God-appointed means of resisting him; (2) because prayer is God's way for us to obtain what we need from him; (3) because the apostles, whom God gave as a pattern for us, considered prayer to be the most important business of their lives; (4) because prayer occupied a very prominent place and played a very important part in the

earthly life of our Lord; (5) because prayer is the most important part of the present ministry of our Lord, since he is now
interceding for us (Heb. 7:25); (6) because prayer is the means
God has appointed for our receiving mercy from him and of
obtaining grace to help in time of need; (7) because prayer
is the means of obtaining the fullness of God's joy; (8) because
prayer with thanksgiving is the means of obtaining freedom
from anxiety and, in anxiety's place, the peace that passes
understanding; (9) because prayer is the method appointed
for obtaining the fullness of God's Holy Spirit; (10) because
prayer is the means by which we are to keep watchful and alert
at Christ's return; and (11) because prayer is used by God to
promote our spiritual growth, bring power into our work,
lead others to faith in Christ and bring all other blessings to
Christ's church.[1]

The Problem of Prayer

In spite of the obvious importance of prayer, most people
misunderstand it and find it confusing. The problem may be
traced to the fact that so few Christians know God well. Since
none of us knows him fully, prayer is at least partially confusing to all of us. Does prayer change things? Or does prayer
change people? Does God change his mind as the result of
believing prayer? Do we move God? Or does God move us to
pray? What does it mean to pray without ceasing? Who can
pray? How should one pray? In any gathering of God's people
many of these questions will receive different and sometimes
even contradictory answers.

Not only do normal people have difficulty with prayer. So
do theologians. At one point in the course of their long and
very influential ministries George Whitefield, the Calvinistic
evangelist, and John Wesley, the Arminian evangelist, were
preaching together in New England. They conducted several
services during the day and returned exhausted to their room
together in a boarding house each night. One evening after a

particularly strenuous day, the two of them returned to prepare for bed. When they were ready each knelt beside his bed to pray. Whitefield, the Calvinist, prayed like this: "Lord, we thank Thee for all those with whom we spoke this day, and we rejoice that their lives and destinies are entirely in thy hand. Honor our efforts according to thy perfect will. Amen." He then climbed in bed.

Wesley, who had hardly gotten past the invocation of his prayer in this length of time, looked up and said, "Mr. Whitefield, is this where your Calvinism leads you?" Then he put his head down again and went on praying.

Whitefield stayed in bed and went to sleep. About two hours later he woke up, and there was Wesley still on his knees beside the bed. Whitefield got up, went around to where Wesley was kneeling and touched him. Wesley was asleep. Whitefield said, "Mr. Wesley, is this where your Arminianism leads you?"

This is not meant to imply that Calvinists inevitably fail to pray simply by virtue of their being Calvinists or that Arminians inevitably fail to pray through human weakness. But it is clear that even the most zealous Christians have difficulties. Calvin believed in God's providence; but in his chapter on prayer, which immediately precedes his chapter on election, he explicitly refutes those who say that God is "vainly importuned with our entreaties."[2] Instead, he speaks of the need to "dig up by prayer" those treasures God has for us.[3] "After we have been instructed by faith to recognize that whatever we need and whatever we lack is in God, and in our Lord Jesus Christ, in whom the Father willed all the fullness of his bounty to abide (cf. Col. 1:19; Jn. 1:16) so that we may all draw from it as from an overflowing spring, it remains for us to seek in him, and in prayers to ask of him, what we have learned to be in him. Otherwise, to know God as the master and bestower of all good things, who invites us to request them of him, and still not go to him and not ask of him—this would be of as little profit as for a man to neglect a treasure, buried and hidden in the earth, after it had been pointed out to him."[4]

Prayer is "digging up" God's treasures. But it is not a way primarily of getting *things* from God, for the treasure about which Calvin speaks includes those riches of grace and glory which are in Christ Jesus.

Prayer–to God

Many of our difficulties in prayer may be removed by getting clear to whom we are praying and what he has done to make prayer possible. This was the point at which our Lord started in his teaching about prayer. In the Sermon on the Mount he began by stressing that the only prayer that can truly be called prayer is that which is directed consciously and explicitly to God the Father. He said, "And when you pray, you must not be like the hypocrites; for they love to stand and pray in the synagogues and at the street corners, that they may be seen by men. Truly, I say to you, they have received their reward. But when you pray, go into your room and shut the door and pray to your Father who is in secret; and your Father who sees in secret will reward you" (Mt. 6:5-6). Jesus is not speaking against the value and practice of public prayer, for the Lord himself prayed publicly (see Jn. 11:41-42). Rather, he is concerned with the tendency we all have to pray to ourselves or others instead of to God. Prayer must always be made to God. It must be made in the knowledge that he is always more ready to answer than we are to pray to him.

Many think that all prayers are offered to God, but that is not the case. It could be argued that not one prayer in a thousand is really offered to the Father of the Lord Jesus Christ. In the world at large, millions of prayers are offered to idols, false gods. In Catholicism many are offered to the saints. In Protestantism many are like the one once uttered in a fashionable Boston church and described afterward as "the most eloquent prayer ever offered to a Boston audience." Obviously the one praying was more concerned with impressing others than with approaching God.

Do my prayers bring me into the presence of God? When I pray, am I really thinking far more of my friends, my busy schedule or what I am asking for than I am of the great God I am approaching? Torrey says that "we should never utter one syllable of prayer either in public or in private until we are definitely conscious that we have come into the presence of God and are actually praying to Him."[5]

Prayer is connected with personal spiritual growth. As the soul grows, the prayer life deepens and vice versa. When children begin praying, for example, there is nothing more than petition. "Now I lay me down to sleep; I pray thee, Lord, my soul to keep," or, "God, bless mommy and daddy and make me a good girl. Amen." Somewhat later, as they grow, they are taught to thank God for things. "Father, I thank you for this food, for rest and play and all good things...." If growth continues, the child is led to consider the needs of others and to think of God and praise him. What happens in the growth of the prayer life of a child should happen in the life of every child of God: from focusing on self to others and then to God. This should reflect and foster spiritual growth.

There is a hymn by Frederick W. Faber, itself a great prayer, whichs looks ahead (in the last stanza) to that fuller spiritual capacity which will only be possible in heaven.

My God, how wonderful Thou art .
Thy majesty how bright!
How beautiful Thy mercy seat,
In depths of burning light!

O how I fear Thee, living God,
With Deepest, tend'rest fears;
And worship Thee with trembling hope,
And penitential tears.

Yet I may love Thee too, O Lord,
  Almighty as Thou art;
For Thou hast stooped to ask of me
  The love of my poor heart.

Father of Jesus, love's reward!
  What rapture will it be,
Prostrate before Thy throne to lie,
  And gaze and gaze on Thee.

In those final words Faber has come to a place which is the spiritual parallel to having fallen in love, when one wants only to be with and gaze upon the beloved.

This movement of prayer—from ourselves to others to God himself—does not stop with God but necessarily returns from him to our own needs and those of others. It is brought about by a new recognition of our sin and weakness, which we always experience when we look on the holy and omnipotent God. This leads to confession of sin. Our concern for others is nourished by the discovery that in his grace God cares for them even as for us. This leads to intercession.

This movement is suggested in the wording of the Lord's Prayer. The prayer begins with God and his interests, as it should. We are instructed to pray, "Our Father who art in heaven, hallowed be *thy* name. *Thy* kingdom come, *thy* will be done, on earth as it is in heaven" (Mt. 6:9-10). This is a prayer for God's honor. But then, no sooner are these petitions outlined, than the prayer goes on, "Give us this day our daily bread; and forgive us our debts, as we also have forgiven our debtors; and lead us not into temptation, but deliver us from evil" (vv. 11-13). By contrast with the first part of the prayer, these are human or earthly concerns. Moreover, the pronouns are not in the singular ("I," "me" or "mine") but in the plural ("we," "us" and "our"). Having seen God in our worship we will inevitably turn back to pray for others.

There is a simple acronym for prayer, which many have

found helpful: ACTS. *A* stands for adoration, *C* for confession, *T* for thanksgiving and *S* for supplication. It suggests that if we have really met with God, we will inevitably confess our sin, thank him for his forgiveness and all other blessings, and intercede for others.

Through Jesus Christ

I pray. But how is this possible? God is holy. How can I, a sinful human being, approach a holy God? True prayer is prayer offered to God the Father on the basis of the death of Jesus Christ. The author of the book of Hebrews puts it like this: "Therefore, brethren, since we have confidence to enter the sanctuary by the blood of Jesus, . . . let us draw near with a true heart in full assurance of faith" (Heb. 10:19, 22). Jesus taught the same thing when he said, "I am the way, and the truth, and the life; no one comes to the Father, but by me" (Jn. 14:6).

If we were to approach God on our own merit, God would have to turn from us. If it were not for Jesus Christ, God would never hear any prayer offered by any human being. However, we can be purified in his sight through faith in Jesus and in this state we may come.

This means, of course, that prayer is for believers only. It is not for the heathen. It is not for the atheist. It is not for the good person who, nevertheless, regards Jesus as nothing more than a man, worth little more than an example.[6]

While God does not hear the prayer of non-Christians, it is also true that he does not hear the prayers offered by many Christians when they cling to some sin. David said, "If I had cherished iniquity in my heart, the Lord would not have listened" (Ps. 66:18). Isaiah wrote, "Behold, the LORD's hand is not shortened, that it cannot save, or his ear dull, that it cannot hear; but your iniquities have made a separation between you and your God, and your sins have hid his face from you so that he does not hear" (Is. 59:1-2). Do these verses describe your prayer life? If so, you must confess your sin openly and frankly, knowing that God "is faithful and just, and will forgive our sins and cleanse us from all unrighteousness" (1 Jn. 1:9).

If I have been dishonest with a friend, it is not very easy for me to talk about anything with him or her. I may be able to force my way through a conversation about the weather, my work or our families. But I do not bring up more personal things. It is only after the air has been cleared between us, after forgiveness has been asked and received, that I am once again able to open up with my friend. It is the same in my relationship with God. If sin keeps me from him, then he is like a stranger and my prayer flows slowly, even though I have believed in Jesus. Instead, I must confess my sin and learn to spend time alone with my heavenly Father. When I do that, my prayer will become the kind of communion that I have in conversation with a close friend.

In the Holy Spirit

Prayer is communion with God the Father through the Lord Jesus Christ. But it is also in the Holy Spirit. Ephesians 2:18 says, "For through him [Jesus] we both have access in one Spirit to the Father." Prayer is coming to God the Father through the Lord Jesus Christ in the Holy Spirit. What does this mean? It is the work of the Holy Spirit to lead us into God's presence, to point God out to us and to make God real when we pray. This is suggested by the Greek word *prosagogē* which is translated "access" in the above verse. Literally it means "an introduction." The Holy Spirit introduces us to God. The Holy Spirit makes God real to us while instructing us how we should pray (Rom. 8:26-27).

Have you ever begun to pray and had the experience that God seems to be far away? If you have, it may be that sin or disobedience to God is hindering you. But it may simply be that things are filling your mind or that worries are obscuring the sense you should have of God's presence. What are you to do in that case? Should you stop and pray again another time? Certainly not, for it is then that you probably need it most. Instead you should be still and, looking to God, ask him to work through his Holy Spirit to make himself real to you and to lead you into his presence. Many Christians find that their most wonderful times of prayer are those in which they start without a clear sense of God's presence but come to it by praying.

If It Be Thy Will

When we approach God as he has told us to approach him, we can have great boldness in prayer, as Wesley, Whitefield, Calvin, Torrey and other great prayer warriors have had. This is what the Lord encouraged in that verse quoted at the beginning of this chapter. "Whatever you ask in my name, I will do it" (Jn. 14:13). This does not mean that we can ask for any foolish or sinful thing and get it. To ask in Christ's name means to ask in accordance with his will. But it does mean that when we ask in accordance with that will we can be confident.

To be faithful to this text, however, we must also say that there are Christians who use the idea of God's will in a way that was never intended and which is not intended here. They use it to save face. Many pray with so little confidence that God will ever answer their prayers that they are constantly adding "if it be thy will" to each of them, as if to say to each other and to themselves that they already know in advance that the thing they are asking for will not happen. Many of these people are deeply astonished when God actually does answer some prayer.

When Herod Antipas was the reigning king in Palestine, the apostle Peter was imprisoned in Jerusalem. The Christians were worried. Peter had been arrested before and released, but Herod had just killed James, the brother of John, and there was every reason to think that he would execute Peter also. The Christians began to pray. They were praying in one part of Jerusalem—at the house of Mary, the mother of John Mark—while God was already at work in another part of the city releasing Peter from prison. The gates were flung open, and an angel led Peter out into the streets of the sleeping city.

We do not know what the Christians at Mary's home were saying. They may have been praying that God would comfort Peter or that God would stay the hand of Herod or, which is more likely, that God would deliver the apostle from prison. But I am sure they were praying "if it be thy will," for they were not expecting God's answer. As they prayed Peter came to the door and knocked. A maid went to see who was there. She was astonished—so much so that she returned to the group who were praying without letting Peter in. But they were worse off than she was, for when they were told that it was Peter, they said, "You are mad." The story continues, "But she insisted that it was so. They said, 'It is his angel!' But Peter continued knocking; and when they opened, they saw him and were amazed. But motioning to them with his hand to be silent, he described to them how the Lord had brought him out of the prison" (Acts 12:15-17).

Many of our prayers are like the prayers of those Christians. In many of our churches prayer has become a duty, and Christians pray without any sure expectation of God's answer. What a pity this is! By contrast Jesus taught that we can live and pray so much in the sphere of God's will that we can be bold in saying, "Thy will be done." We may ask in confidence, knowing that God's will shall be done in our lives and churches.

It was a sense of being in the center of God's will that gave Luther his great boldness in prayer. In 1540, Luther's great friend and assistant, Frederick Myconius, became sick and was expected to die within a short time. Luther received the letter and instantly sent back a reply. "I command thee in the name of God to live because I still have need of thee in the work of reforming the church. . . . The Lord will never let me hear that thou art dead, but will permit thee to survive me. For this I am praying, this is my will, and may my will be done, because I seek only to glorify the name of God." The words are almost shocking to us for we live in a more sensitive and cautious day, but they were certainly from God. For although Myconius had already lost the ability to speak when Luther's letter came, in a short time he revived. He recovered completely, and he lived six more years to survive Luther himself by two months.[7]

We are never so bold in prayer as when we can look in the face of God and say, "My Father, I do not pray for myself in this thing, and I do not want my will done. I want thy name to be glorified. Glorify it now in my situation, in my life, and do it in such a way that all will know it is of thee."[8]

15

GOD TALKING TO US

Dwight L. Moody once said, "In prayer we talk to God. In Bible study, God talks to us, and we had better let God do most of the talking."[1] The Bible stresses the importance of Bible study too. In the first psalm David speaks of Bible study as the essential source of blessing in the religious life: "Blessed is the man who walks not in the counsel of the wicked, nor stands in the way of sinners, nor sits in the seat of scoffers; but his delight is in the law of the LORD, and on his law he meditates day and night. He is like a tree planted by streams of water, that yields its fruit in its season, and its leaf does not wither. In all that he does, he prospers" (Ps. 1:1-3). In Psalm 119, the author speaks of Bible study as the secret of holy living: "How can a young man keep his way pure? By guarding it according to thy word. . . . I have laid up thy word in my heart, that I might not sin against thee" (Ps. 119:9, 11). In the New Testament Paul speaks of Bible study as the key to becoming equipped for Christian service: "All scripture is inspired by God and profitable for teaching, for reproof, for correction, and for training in righteousness, that the man of God may be complete, equipped for every good work" (2 Tim. 3:16-17).

"You Search the Scriptures"
Unfortunately, human beings have a knack for abusing the gifts of God. Bishop John C. Ryle of Liverpool says that Christendom as a whole has neglected and abused the Bible. He observed that in his day there were more Bibles and there had been more Bible selling and distribution than at any previous period of Christian history. Yet many if not most who possessed the Bible simply did not read it.[2] That is not something uniquely characteristic of England in the latter half of the nineteenth century, however. It is a characteristic of our day also. We have billions of Bibles in many scores of translations. Yet millions scarcely read God's Word. Instead, they allow activities to surfeit their lives and stunt their souls.

The Bible is sometimes misused in other ways as well. One way in which it is misused is to consider it an end in itself and thus fail to allow it to accomplish its primary purpose—to lead us to a knowledge of God through faith in Jesus Christ. Sometimes this happens in biblical scholarship. The nineteenth-century "historical Jesus" movement is an example. This movement was a century-long attempt to get behind the Jesus of the New Testament, who was regarded as the faith-product of the early church, to the actual historical Jesus who was to be stripped of all "unhistorical" supernatural elements. This effort was prodigious, but it produced nothing lasting. In failing to be led by the Bible to the true, New Testament Jesus, scholars succeeded only in producing a Jesus made in their own image. Rationalists discovered him to be a great teacher of ethics. Socialists viewed him as a revolutionary. Radicals, such as Bruno Bauer, denied that he even existed. At length Albert Schweitzer put an end to the search with his devastating critique in *The Quest of the Historical Jesus*.[3] Scholarship had made the Gospels an end in themselves. The Bible had become a book to be weighed and manipulated rather than to be believed and obeyed.

We may have something similar in the evangelicals' use of translations. Clearly, translations are necessary (for few Christians know Greek and Hebrew, the original languages of the Bible), and a good, accurate, contemporary translation is invaluable in any serious program of Bible study. But at times there is an unfortunate and unhealthy preoccupation with the "best" or "latest" or "most contemporary" translation which titillates our interest but does little to actually get us into the principles of God's Word and produce obedience to them. The small variations between different texts prove more interesting than the teaching itself. In this way obedience to Christ and a desire to know him better are sidelined.

I believe that there is no need for another English translation in our day. We have all varieties. Any taste can be satisfied. I even believe that much of our current interest in translations is traceable to the publishers who encourage it for commercial purposes. The immense amounts of effort expended on producing such translations would be far better spent in getting the Bible into the languages of men and women who have not yet seen even one version of the Scriptures.

In light of these problems, Jesus' warning to the Jews of his day is quite relevant. He said, "You search the scriptures, because you think that in them you have eternal life; and it is they that bear witness to me; yet you refuse to come to me that you may have life" (Jn. 5:39-40).

No one could fault the Jews for their meticulous study of the Scriptures. The scribes, whose work it was to copy the scrolls, subjected the pages of the Bible to the closest scrutiny. They gave attention to every syllable. They even counted the words and letters so that they knew which came in the middle of the page and how many of each a given page should have. We can be thankful for this care in one sense, for the accuracy of our present Old Testament texts is a result. Nevertheless, in most cases the reaction of the scribe to the Word of God stopped with the copying. And those who used their texts, being possessed of the same mentality, looked at the finest points but missed the Bible's message. The words were accurate, but what is the value of these without meanings? What is the value of letters if these are not inscribed on an obedient heart?

Many who are reading this book have a high degree of biblical knowledge. You can name the twelve apostles, the cities Paul visited and perhaps even the Hebrew kings. But have you missed what the Scriptures have to teach about sin (your sin), justification (your justification), the Christian life (your Christian life) and obedience (your obedience)?

Studying the Bible

The importance of the Bible and the proper approach to Bible study arise from what the Bible is: the very Word of God. That the Bible is "inspired by God" (2 Tim. 3:16) makes it utterly unlike any other book ever written by any man or woman. While the Bible is also a human product, God taught the writers what to say and guided them in their writing. The result? Precisely what God desired to be written.

When we read the Bible we are not reading the thoughts of men and women like ourselves, which may or may not be true. Rather, we are reading the word of God to us. And just because it is the Word of *God*, we cannot read it and be indifferent or unchanged. Ryle writes, "When you read [the Bible], you are not reading the self-taught compositions of poor imperfect men like yourself, but the words of the eternal God. When you hear it, you are not listening to the erring opinions of short-lived mortals, but to the unchanging mind of the King of kings. The men who were employed to indite the Bible spoke not of themselves. They 'spake as they were moved by the Holy Ghost' (2 Pet. 1:21). All other books in the world, however good and useful in their way, are more or less defective. The more you look at them the more you see their defects and blemishes. The Bible alone is absolutely perfect. From beginning to end it is 'the Word of God.' "[4]

But the Bible is not remote, impersonal information which dropped in from outer space. The living God continues to speak to his people through it. So we approach the Bible devotionally, as though it were a holy place where we meet and have fellowship with God.

God speaks in Scripture through the Holy Spirit. That is why the subject of Bible study reoccurs here, in volume three of this series, rather than being exhausted in volume one. In volume one I considered the role of the Spirit primarily in the inspiration of the Bible. Here I discuss his role in teaching us from what he inspired. Paul writes in 1 Corinthians that in ourselves we are unable to understand spiritual truth even when it is recorded in the pages of the Word of God. But the Spirit of truth speaks to us from its pages to bring understanding.

> *As it is written, "What no eye has seen, nor ear heard, nor the heart of man conceived, what God has prepared for those who love him," God has revealed to us through the Spirit. For the Spirit searches everything, even the depths of God. For what person knows a man's thoughts except the spirit of the man which is in him? So also no one comprehends the thoughts of God except the Spirit of God. Now we have received not the spirit of the world, but the Spirit which is from God, that we might understand the gifts bestowed on us by God. And we impart this in words not taught by human wisdom but taught by the Spirit, interpreting spiritual truths to those who possess the Spirit. (1 Cor. 2:9-13)*

"What is the right way to study the Bible?" There are those who confess that the Bible is the Word of God and who want to meet the living God in its pages but who perhaps are not quite sure how to go about it. Here are five answers to their important question.

1. Study the Bible daily (Acts 17:11). Certainly we can turn to the Bible more than once each day or, equally, there may be occasions when legitimate concerns consume the daily time we would normally spend studying. But we should discipline our lives to include a daily period of Bible study, just as we discipline ourselves to have regular periods for sleep, for brushing our teeth, for meals and so on. In fact, the comparison with regular mealtimes is a good one for these are necessary if the body is to be healthy and if good work is to be done. On occasion we may miss a meal, but normally we should not. In the same way, we must feed regularly on God's Word if we are to become and remain spiritually strong.

What happens if we neglect such daily Bible reading? We grow indifferent to God and lax in spiritual things. We throw ourselves open to temptation and the sin which can easily follow.

The regular time we set aside for Bible study may be long— for those who are mature in the faith and who have time for such study, perhaps an hour or two. It may be shorter—for those who are new in the faith or who lead tight schedules, perhaps only ten or fifteen minutes. Whatever the length of time, it should be fixed and at a set period of the day.

When should this be? Again this may vary from person to person. Many have found that the best time is at the very beginning of the day. Torrey writes, "Wherever it is possible, the best time for this study is immediately after arising in the morning. The worst time of all is the last thing at night. Of course, it is well to spend a little while Bible reading just before we retire, in order that God's voice may be the last to which we listen, but the bulk of our Bible study should be done at an hour when our minds are clearest and strongest. Whatever time is set apart for Bible study should be kept sacredly for that purpose."[5]

2. Study the Bible systematically. Some people read the Bible at random, dipping here or there. This may be characteristic of the way they do most things in life, but it is a mistake in Bible study (as well as in most other things). It inevitably leads to a lack of proportion and depth which is so often characteristic of Christians today. A far better system is a regular, disciplined study of certain books of the Bible or even of the Bible as a whole. New Christians could begin with one of the Gospels, perhaps the Gospel of John or Mark. After this they could go on to Acts, Ephesians, Galatians, Romans or an Old Testament book such as Genesis. It is always valuable to read and meditate on the Psalms.

Certain procedures should be followed during study. First, the book itself should be read through carefully as many as four or five times, perhaps one of these times aloud. Each time something new will strike you.

Second, divide the book into its chief sections, just as we divide modern books into chapters (not necessarily the same chapters as in our Bibles), subsections and paragraphs. At this stage the object should be to see which verses belong together, what subjects are covered and what the sequence of subjects is.

Third, these sections should be related to one another: Which are the main sections or subjects? Which are introductory? Which are excursuses? Applications? At this stage one should be developing an outline of the book and should be able to answer such questions as, What does this book say? To whom was it written? Why was it written? If you were studying Romans, for example, you should be able to say, "This book was written to the church at Rome, but also to churches in all places and at all times. It says that the human race is lost in sin and that the answer to that sin is the righteousness of God revealed in Jesus Christ. Its purpose is to explain this gospel. A minor purpose was to alert the Romans to Paul's desire to visit them on his way to a future ministry in Spain."

You can now proceed to a more detailed study of the individual sections. What is the main subject of each section? What is said about it? Why is it said? To whom? What are the conclusions that follow from it? It is helpful in this study to watch the small connecting words like *but, because, then, and, since* and *therefore.*

Last, you can study key words. How do you go about it? Begin by looking at other passages in the same book in which the word occurs. You can find these by your own reading or by using a concordance in which important verses containing such words are listed. Simple concordances are in the back of many Bibles.

Suppose you were studying Romans 3:21-26 and wanted to learn more about the important word *righteousness,* with which the section begins. One key verse is 10:3, in which the righteousness of God is distinguished from our righteousness. Also, Romans 1:17 says that the righteousness of God is made known in the gospel. In all, *righteousness* is used thirty-five times in this one letter alone, and most of these uses throw light on one another. At this point you may also observe the use of the word in other books of the Bible, perhaps using the chain-reference system which some Bibles provide. You can also use the dictionary. Some large dictionaries contain the derivations of words, which also throw light on their meanings.

Normally it is only at the end of a personal, inductive system of Bible study such as this that the comments of others on the text should be considered. Where these are used, good commentaries on individual books of the Bible will generally be found more helpful than skimpier one-volume commentaries on the whole of the Old and New Testaments.

3. Study the Bible comprehensively. Alongside serious, in-depth study of one book or section of the Bible, there should also be an attempt to become acquainted with the whole Bible. This means reading it comprehensively. True, many parts of the Bible will not appeal to us at first. This is natural. But if we never make an attempt to become acquainted with them, we limit our growth and may even warp our understanding.

Paul told Timothy, "*All* scripture is inspired by God and profitable for teaching, for reproof, for correction, and for training in righteousness" (2 Tim. 3:16, my emphasis).

Ryle's testimony on this point is that "it is by far the best plan to begin the Old and New Testaments at the same time—to read each straight through to the end, and then begin again." He acknowledges that this is a matter of individual preference, but he says, "I can only say it has been my own plan for nearly forty years, and I have never seen cause to alter it."[6]

4. Study the Bible prayerfully. Doing this provides the remedy for studying the Bible for its own sake, discussed earlier in this chapter. By prayer we can avoid the mere formalism of the scribes. In true Bible study we first ask the Holy Spirit to open our minds to understand his truth and then obey it as he applies it to our lives.

The author of Psalm 119 indicates the proper attitude when he writes, "Deal bountifully with thy servant, that I may live and observe thy word. Open my eyes, that I may behold wondrous things out of thy law" (vv. 17-18). What will a prayer like this accomplish? It makes us conscious that we are actually meeting with God in our reading and not merely going through some prescribed religious ritual. After we pray we must say to ourselves, "God is now going to speak to me," and then we must read to hear what he will say. There is probably nothing that will make Bible study more exciting than this—to know that as we read God is actually speaking to us personally and is teaching us. This makes Bible study and the prayer that accompanies it a time of personal communion with him.

5. Finally, *study the Bible obediently.* Earlier I suggested a number of questions that should be asked if we want to understand a given passage of Scripture. But in that list some of the most important questions were left out. How does this passage and its teachings apply to me? Does this instruct me in something I should do? In something I should not do? What does it tell me about the will of God and how I can please God and serve him better? James had this in mind when he instructed those to whom he was writing, "But be doers of the word, and not hearers only, deceiving yourselves" (Jas. 1:22).

God requires obedience. If he instructs us, it is so we will obey him and grow. What should we do? "Cultivate prompt, exact, unquestioning, joyous obedience to every command that it is evident from its context applies to you. Be on the lookout for new orders from your King. Blessing lies in the direction of obedience to them. God's commands are but signboards that mark the road to present success and blessedness and to eternal glory."[7] If we are not willing to obey God, we will not even understand what we read (Jn. 7:17) and Bible study will become dull, oppressive and meaningless. We will even drift away from God and find ourselves criticizing his Word. We will find ourselves susceptible to critical theories which demean it. But if we are willing to obey, God will help us understand his truths and lead us to others as well.

One writer has observed, "Serious Bible study does not consist merely in digging into the Word, but it demands a translation of that Word through our lives to the world. We are to be God's epistles read of all men. . . . If we take our Bible study seriously, to the extent that we will obey him, then we shall discover the way of real spiritual blessing, and we shall be successful men of God for our Lord Jesus Christ."[8]

16   SERVING

Michael once wrote me to ask advice on how to remain a strong Christian during his years in college. He was in his first year at Harvard University to which he had come from the Midwest. He was worried that pressures of study and the dominant secular viewpoint in many fields might undermine his faith. As I thought, three things came to mind. So I wrote that he should arrange his schedule to provide for these elements: (1) a period of daily Bible study and prayer; (2) regular fellowship and worship with other Christians, both with his peers (perhaps in a dorm Bible study or in some other student meeting of Christians and in a weekly church service; and (3) some form of regular service to others. I suggested that this last point could take many forms: an outreach to non-Christians, a tutoring project for the disadvantaged or social service work, for example. Only in such activity do we get our minds off ourselves and onto others and their problems, as Christ indicated we should do if we are to be his disciples (Phil. 2:4).

If we neglect such works, we will inevitably be impoverished. Reuben A. Torrey once put it, "If you wish to be a happy Christian, if you wish to be a strong Christian, if you wish to be a Christian who is mighty in prayer, begin at once to work for the Master and never let a day pass without doing some definite work for him."[1]

"Not Me, Lord!"
Ephesians 2:10 occurs at the end of a series of well-known verses explaining how we are saved by the grace of God through faith, not works. But this passage immediately goes on to say quite practically, "For we are his workmanship, created in Christ Jesus for good works, which God prepared beforehand [the KJV says 'ordained'], that we should walk in them." God has a plan for every individual Christian's life and good works are in that plan. Yet our insensitivity to God's plan or our laziness is so great that we constantly try to evade this obligation.

Some try to evade it theologically. They stress justification by grace through faith, apart from works, to such an extent that our obligation to do good works evaporates. For example, one of the most thorough treatments of Ephesians 2 in print today is a four-hundred-page analysis in which twenty-four pages are given to an examination of verses 8-10. But this key phrase dealing with our ordination to good works receives only one paragraph of exposition.

While justification by faith, apart from works, is certainly biblical teaching, as we saw in chapter seven, this does not mean that there is no place for good works if one is justified. Ephesians 2:8-10 itself makes this strikingly clear because the word *works* occurs twice—once as that which God curses and once as that which God blesses. In verse 9 we are told that salvation is "not because of works, lest any man should boast." These are works which arise out of our own nature and which we might trust for salvation. But immediately after this Paul speaks of those "works" which God has appointed to be done by those who are justified.

Another attempt to evade our obligation to do good works is spiritual. Some take it to mean the good, spiritual things we know we should do as Christians—pray, read the Bible, witness. While these aspects of the Christian life are indeed valuable, they are not really "good works" in the sense that Paul is speaking. If Paul was thinking of witnessing, for example, he would have said that God has ordained us to be witnesses.

The third way in which the implication of Ephesians 2:10 is avoided is organizational. How often we stress our immense social programs and plans for social action! It seems strange to say that an emphasis on evangelical social action, which is greatly needed and long overdue in our generation can actually stifle good works. But it happens quite simply. People hear of these problems, are impressed with their scope, conclude that the only way they can ever adequately be dealt with is by massive organizational effort and then wrongly neglect the good they can do as individuals.

We need good theology. We need prayer, Bible study and other elements of a healthy Christian life and ministry. We must establish and support effective social action programs. But these do not replace being doers of good works individually. Apart from the life and ministry of Jesus himself, Christians are to be the best thing that ever happened to this world. We are to be sources of constant good, sharing, love and service so that the world might be blessed and some (we do not forget this) might come to faith in our Savior.

The Lord pointed to this need in the Sermon on the Mount when he called his followers "the salt of the earth" and "the light of the world." Salt is good and light is valued. So let your saltiness be tasted and your light seen, he argued. And do this that the world "may see your good works and give glory to your Father who is in heaven" (Mt. 5:13-16).

The Compassion of Christ

What Jesus prescribed for others he did no less himself. Today we tend to focus on his teaching and marvel at it, as people also did in his own day (Mt. 7:28-29). But when we read the Gospels with the subject of good works in mind, we are immediately impressed with how major a part of Christ's ministry doing good was.

This was the note on which Jesus began his ministry when reading from the scroll of Isaiah in the synagogue at Nazareth. He had been asked to take part in the service by leading a lesson for the day. So he turned to that part of Isaiah's prophecy concerning the coming of the Messiah that says, "The Spirit of the Lord is upon me, because he has anointed me to preach good news to the poor. He has sent me to proclaim release to the captives and recovering of sight to the blind, to set at liberty those who are oppressed, to proclaim the acceptable year of the Lord" (Lk. 4:18-19; quoting Is. 61: 1-2). This has overtones of a spiritual ministry, of course, for eyes were opened to truth and captives to sin were set free. But that is not the whole of the matter, as the remainder of the chapter shows. The second half of Luke 4 records the beginning of Christ's miracles: the casting out of demons and the healing of Peter's mother-in-law. It then says, "Now when the sun was setting, all those who had any that were sick with various diseases brought them to him; and he laid his hands on every one of them and healed them" (v. 40).

Again, when John the Baptist was in prison and began to have doubts about Jesus being the Messiah, he sent disciples to ask Jesus about it. Jesus referred to this same passage and directed John to consider the healing of the blind, lame, deaf and lepers that Jesus had done as the prophecy's fulfillment.

These works were not just done to get people to believe in him either. He simply had compassion for those who were sick, hungry or needy. Not all he healed believed, at least we are not told that they did. Not all were even friends. He healed the ear of the servant of the high priest who had come to arrest him in the garden of Gethsemane and who had been attacked by Peter in a misguided attempt to save Jesus (Lk. 22: 50-51). He taught that good should be done even to our enemies by reminding us that God "makes his sun rise on the evil and on the good, and sends rain on the just and on the unjust" (Mt. 5:45). In the parable of the good Samaritan he taught that good should be done even to those who are culturally despised (Lk. 10:30-37).

It was not just miraculous works that Jesus performed either. If that were true, we might conclude that true good works are beyond us. Apparently, the Lord and his disciples kept a fund out of which they gave to those who were needy (Jn. 13:29).

Jesus also encouraged others to do good works. He noticed a poor widow putting two small copper coins, which together only added up to a penny, in the temple poor box. "This poor widow," he said, "has put in more than all those who are contributing to the treasury. For they all contributed out of their abundance; but she out of her poverty has put in everything she had, her whole living" (Mk. 12:43-44). On the other hand, Mary of Bethany broke a box of costly ointment to anoint his feet just before his arrest and crucifixion. Judas and perhaps others objected, but he replied, "Let her alone; why do you trouble her? She has done a beautiful thing to me. For you always have the poor with you, and whenever you will, you can do good to them; but you will not always have me" (Mk. 14:6-7). And when Zacchaeus was converted and promised to give half of his goods to the poor and repay fourfold any he had cheated, Jesus responded, "Today salvation has come to this house" (Lk. 19:9).

This World's Salt
Our Lord demonstrated as well as taught that good works

should be characteristic of all his followers. And this has been so throughout church history. Many things characterized the early Christian communities, of course; but they were noted for being generous and caring for one another and for the poor. After about three thousand were saved following Peter's great speech at Pentecost, we are told that "all who believed were together and had all things in common; and they sold their possessions and goods and distributed them to all, as any had need" (Acts 2:44-45). After the church had increased even further, it is recorded that "there was not a needy person among them, for as many as were possessors of lands or houses sold them, and brought the proceeds of what was sold and laid it at the apostles' feet; and distribution was made to each as any had need" (Acts 4:34-35).

This selling of goods and holding of all things in common does not overturn the right of private property. This right is recognized in Acts 5:4. But this was a generous church all the same. Other churches were also generous in other ways.

In Acts 6 we are told of the choice of the first church officers (apart from the apostles who were picked and commissioned by Christ). The duties of these deacons, as they were called, were to care for the sick and poor, and to distribute goods to them as they had need (Acts 6:1-6). Among these was Stephen, the first martyr.

In a later chapter of Acts we are told of Dorcas who "was full of good works and acts of charity" (Acts 9:36). When she died there was great mourning and all the widows whom she had helped came "weeping, and showing tunics and other garments which Dorcas made while she was with them" (v. 39). Peter raised Dorcas from the dead. Another person noted for good works in Acts 9 was Simon the tanner who was a resident of Joppa. He made his house available to Peter when Peter was in the city. In the next chapter Cornelius, the Roman centurion, is praised as one who "gave alms liberally to the people, and prayed constantly to God," even before his conversion

(Acts 10:2). In Acts 12 we are introduced to Mary, the mother of John Mark, who made her house available for Christian meetings, in this case an all-night prayer meeting (v. 12).

Several times in Acts we read of collections being taken to aid the poor. On one occasion this was done in response to a famine in Jerusalem (Acts 11:27-30). On another, it was an offering from the gentile churches to the Jerusalem poor (Acts 24:17; compare 1 Cor. 16:1-4; 2 Cor. 8:1—9:5).

Apparently, the charitable instincts of the early church carried over into the period of the apologists, for they often pointed to the goodness of Christians as part of their defense of the faith. The Athenian philosopher Aristides wrote this about Christians to Hadrian:

They do not commit adultery or immorality; they do not bear false witness, or embezzle, nor do they covet what is not theirs. They honor father and mother, and do good to those who are their neighbors. Whenever they are judges, they judge uprightly. They do not worship idols made in the image of man. Whatever they do not wish that others should do to them, they in turn do not do; and they do not eat the food sacrificed to idols. Those who oppress them they exhort and make them their friends. They do good to their enemies. Their wives, O King, are pure as virgins, and their daughters are modest. Their men abstain from all unlawful sexual contact and from impurity, in the hope of recompense that is to come in another world. . . . They love one another; the widow's needs are not ignored, and they rescue the orphan from the person who does him violence. He who has gives to him who has not, ungrudgingly and without boasting. When the Christians find a stranger, they bring him to their homes and rejoice over him as a true brother. They do not call brothers those who are bound by blood ties alone, but those who are brethren after the Spirit and in God. When one of their poor passes away from the world, each provides for his burial according to his ability. If they hear of any of their number who are imprisoned or oppressed for the name of the Messiah, they all provide for his needs, and if it is possible to redeem him, they set him

*free. If they find poverty in their midst, and they do not have spare
food, they fast two or three days in order that the needy might be
supplied with the necessities.* [2]

As Christianity made its way in the Roman world, the impact
of its compassion was felt. The cruel sports of the arena were
checked. Laws were passed to protect slaves, prisoners and
women. The exposure of infants was outlawed. Hospitals
and orphanages were founded. The status of underprivileged
people was upgraded. The progress was not always constant.
But this was the general direction.

The same concerns were particularly evident during the
Reformation and in the modern missionary movement. The
missionary movement established hospitals and schools
literally around the world. Even today many leaders in nearly
every independent nation of Africa acknowledge receiving
their early training and motivation to serve their country in
mission schools.

What of today? The situation is confused by the prolifera-
tion of government services. Social security, Medicare, un-
employment and various other social programs pre-empt
what many Christians did previously, doing it better in total
resources but not necessarily better in compassion or person-
alized care. Yet there are ample opportunities for those who
are alert to the need to do good works. Groups of Christians,
such as those meeting weekly in home Bible studies, are particularly effective. I have watched Bible study groups in my
own church help people move from one apartment to another
or from an apartment to a retirement home. Some have taken
turns staying overnight in a home where someone was sick
and needed care. They have collected food for those in need,
including some inner-city Christian workers. They have collected clothing, given blood, cleaned apartments, transported
the sick to hospitals for care or treatment and done other such
things. Many simply work hard in jobs through which others
are benefited.

To God Be the Glory

Throughout history Christians have truly been "the salt of the earth" in precisely the way their Lord envisioned when he instructed them to do good works. Yet this has not always been the case. If we are to be ruthlessly truthful, we have probably fallen particularly short in our own generation. Christians are no longer especially known as those who do good to others. Some of us seldom do anything particularly good for anybody.

It is easier to serve ourselves, of course. But we must not. First, the presence of good works in a Christian's life is one evidence of salvation. We now think differently than we did before our conversion and seek to serve others in ways that would never have occurred to us before. Here is evidence that we are new creatures in Christ. In chapter eight I said that a practical expression of love for others is one proof of new life presented by the apostle John. "We know that we have passed out of death into life, because we love the brethren" (1 Jn. 3:14).

Second, doing good works is a means of growth in the Christian life. If we desire this, we should serve others faithfully. What happens if we do not? We become introverted, selfish, insensitive and mean. When we do good to others our horizons are broadened, we grow in soul and become more and more like Jesus.

Third (and how self-evident), good works are a blessing to those we serve. It is hard to put ourselves in the place of others, particularly when they are needy and we are well off. But we must remember that whatever our failures in this regard may be, they are not the failures of our Lord. He considers service to others as service to himself. "Then the King will say to those at his right hand, 'Come, O blessed of my Father, inherit the kingdom prepared for you from the foundation of the world; for I was hungry and you gave me food, I was thirsty and you gave me drink, I was a stranger and you welcomed me. I was naked and you clothed me, I was sick and you visited me, I was in prison and you came to me' " (Mt. 25:34-36). Jesus is blessed through our service to others; and if he is, so are they.

Finally, God is glorified by our works. Only through his life within and by his grace are we able to do them. Some may ask, "If justification is not by works, what value do they have? And why does the Bible sometimes speak of 'rewards' for good works if these are not meritorious?" Calvin answers:

> There is no doubt that whatever is praiseworthy in works is God's grace; there is not a drop that we ought by rights to ascribe to ourselves. If we truly and earnestly recognize this, not only will all confidence in merit vanish, but the very notion. We are not dividing the credit for good works between God and man, as the Sophists do, but we are preserving it whole, complete, and unimpaired for the Lord. To man we may assign only this: that he pollutes and contaminates by his impurity those very things which are good. For nothing proceeds from a man, however perfect he be, that is not defiled by some spot. Let the Lord, then, call to judgment the best in human works: he will indeed recognize in them his own righteousness but man's dishonor and shame! Good works, then, are pleasing to God and are not unfruitful for their doers. But they receive by way of reward the most ample benefits of God, not because they so deserve but because God's kindness has of itself set this value on them.[3]

If our chief end is "to glorify God, and to enjoy him forever," as the Westminster Shorter Catechism suggests, the doing of good works is obviously one way to fulfill the first part.

PART IV
THE WORK OF GOD

We know that in everything God works for good with those who love him, who are called according to his purpose. For those whom he foreknew he also predestined to be conformed to the image of his Son, in order that he might be the first-born among many brethren. And those whom he predestined he also called; and those whom he called he also justified; and those whom he justified he also glorified. (Romans 8:28-30)

I am sure that he who began a good work in you will bring it to completion at the day of Jesus Christ. (Philippians 1:6)

"Deliverance belongs to the LORD!" (Jonah 2:9)

17 CALLED BY GOD

It is often pointed out that Calvin does not discuss the doctrine of election, for which he is noted, at the beginning of his *Institutes* but rather toward the end of book three, that is, about three-quarters of the way through. Calvin did not start with some rigid preconception as to how God must have operated in saving the human race. Rather, he began as a biblical theologian, teaching what God actually has done. Only after that did he look back to see the matter in its fullest perspective: that on the one hand, salvation begins in eternity past in God's determination to save a people for himself and that, on the other hand, it continues into the eternal future, in God's final perseverance with his saints. I am going to follow the same procedure in these last two chapters.

God of Beginnings
In the book of Jonah, at the end of the prophet's great prayer of deliverance there is the sentence: "Salvation is of the LORD" (2:9 KJV). This sentence is simple and profound. The origin,

the end and, indeed, the only possible source of salvation is God. Salvation begins with God's choice of us rather than our choice of him and continues to a successful conclusion because God perseveres with us. Jonah's case is a perfect example. God elected him to do a work that he did not want to do: the evangelization of Nineveh. God persevered with Jonah in spite of the rebellious prophet's attempts to run away.

Though Jonah's call was to a particular ministry and not to salvation, the principle is the same. For nothing can take place spiritually in a person's life until God on the basis of his own determination calls that person to him. It would be foolish for a preacher to enter a funeral home to encourage the corpses to lead an upright life. The corpses are dead. If the words are to have any purpose, the corpses must first be made alive. After that they can respond. In the same way, the call to discipleship must begin with the act of God in making a spiritually dead person alive. The choice to do that is not with the one who is spiritually dead but with God who alone is able to give life.

This is what new birth means. Before conversion, God says we are dead in trespasses and sins. We are alive physically and intellectually, but not spiritually. We cannot respond to spiritual stimuli. The Word of God is a hidden book; the gospel is nonsense. But then God touches us. He brings life out of death. We then believe in Jesus Christ and begin to understand the Bible. This is what it means to be called by God, and this must happen before there can be any true discipleship. Jesus said, "You did not choose me, but I chose you and appointed you that you should go and bear fruit and that your fruit should abide" (Jn. 15:16).

Abraham was called. He did not choose God. He was apparently perfectly satisfied being where he was in the Mesopotamian river valley in a pagan culture. But God called him and sent him on his way to Palestine.

Moses was called even before he was a baby floating in the

Nile in a basket. God said, "I am going to deliver my people from Egypt, and I am going to do it by means of this baby. I am going to protect him from Pharaoh. I am going to give him the best of the world's training and education, and then I am going to use him. I am going to send him to Pharaoh to say, 'Let my people go.' "

It was the same with David. God put his stamp on the future king while David was still out protecting some sheep. God sent the prophet Samuel to David's home to anoint one of the sons in the family as the future king, but when Samuel arrived David was missing. The father brought out all his sons except David. They were there in order. Samuel looked at the boys and thought how good a king the oldest son would make. His name was Eliab. But before Samuel could anoint him God indicated that he was not the one. Next came Abinadab, who was not the future king either. Then there was Shammah, and so on until seven of Jesse's sons were presented.

Samuel said, "The LORD has not chosen these." Then he asked, "Are all your sons here?"

Jesse replied, "There remains yet the youngest, but behold, he is keeping the sheep."

Samuel said, "Send and fetch him; for we will not sit down till he comes here."

When David had come, the Lord said, "Arise, anoint him; for this is he." The Bible continues the account by saying, "Then Samuel took the horn of oil, and anointed him in the midst of his brothers; and the Spirit of the LORD came mightily upon David from that day forward" (1 Sam. 16:10-13). It was God who called David.

In the New Testament God chose John the Baptist—even before he was born. Jesus called his disciples while they were still fishermen. God called Paul when he was in the process of persecuting Christians. In every case the call of God was primary, and this in turn was based on God's own determination to save and use that one.

God's Purpose

Not only do examples help us understand this doctrine. There is also the specific teaching of Scripture. One key passage, indeed one of the most important passages of all, is Romans 8:28-30 in which the election and calling of God are put in a carefully expressed sequence of acts. "We know that in everything God works for good with those who love him, who are called according to his purpose. For those whom he foreknew he also predestined to be conformed to the image of his Son, in order that he might be the first-born among many brethren. And those whom he predestined he also called; and those whom he called he also justified; and those whom he justified he also glorified."

These verses do not contain every step that might possibly be listed in God's dealings with an individual. Nothing is said of regeneration, adoption or sanctification. Yet although this is a truncated list, it is an orderly list that gives a proper sequence to God's actions.

In part two of this book, I considered the application of salvation by the Holy Spirit. But this is only the second half of God's work. A prior determination of God precedes our awakening and spiritual growth. This is expressed in the words *his purpose, foreknew* and *predestined.* The next term in the sequence, *called,* is the point at which this eternal determination passes over into the experience of the individual. The overall term is *purpose,* an eternal purpose expressed first in foreknowledge and predestination (v. 29) and then, as a follow-up to that, in calling, justification and glorification. The remainder of the passage shows that this work of God is certain of completion. For nothing "will be able to separate us from the love of God in Christ Jesus our Lord" (v. 39).

Use of the word *foreknow* has led some to argue that election is based on foreknowledge in the sense that God foresaw that certain people would be more responsive to the gospel than others and would therefore yield to the Holy Spirit where others would not. As a consequence he predestined those who would yield to salvation. These thoughts are wrong if for no other reason than simply because the passage does not start with the idea of foreknowledge but rather with a statement of God's purpose to save. Arthur W. Pink writes that this wrong thinking also "repudiates the truth of total depravity, for it argues that there is something good in some men. It takes away the independency of God, for it makes his decrees rest upon what he discovered in the creature. It completely turns things upside down, for in saying that God foresaw certain sinners would believe in Christ, and that because of this, he predestinated them unto salvation, it is the very reverse of the truth. Scripture affirms that God, in his high sovereignty, singled out certain ones to be recipients of his distinguishing favors (Acts 13:48), and therefore he determined to bestow upon them the gift of faith."[1]

The debate can be ended by answering, What does the word *foreknowledge* mean in Scripture? If *I* said I had foreknowledge, I would mean I had advance information of something that was going to happen. Having this I could take some particular action. But God is not a creature of time as we are. We should also note that the simpler word *know* is characteristically used in the Old and New Testaments to mean "to look upon with favor" or even "to love."

"And the LORD said to Moses, 'This very thing that you have spoken I will do; for you have found favor in my sight, and I know you by name' " (Ex. 33:17). "You only have I known of all the families of the earth; therefore I will punish you for all your iniquities" (Amos 3:2). "Then will I declare to them, 'I never knew you; depart from me, you evildoers' " (Mt. 7:23). "I am the good shepherd; I know my own and my own know me" (Jn. 10:14). "If one loves God, one is known by him" (1 Cor. 8:3). "God's firm foundation stands, bearing this seal: 'The Lord knows those who are his' " (2 Tim. 2:19).

The word *foreknowledge* itself is never used in reference to events or actions—that is, as advance knowledge of what one would or might do—but always of persons, whose lives are affected by that foreknowledge rather than the other way around.

Aside from Romans, there are only three passages in Scripture where the word *foreknowledge* is used, and they all involve the idea of election. The first is Acts 2:23. "This Jesus, delivered up according to the definite plan and foreknowledge of God, you crucified and killed by the hands of lawless men." In this verse it is not the crucifixion which was foreknown by God (though, of course, he did foreknow it in our sense of the word as well), but rather Jesus himself. The verse teaches that God had fixed a plan as a result of which we would be saved and that Jesus was elected to implement that plan.

Romans 11:2 is the second passage. "God has not rejected his people whom he foreknew." Again, it is a people and not their actions that are said to be the object of God's foreknowledge. In spite of what appears to be the case in some instances, none of those who are the elect of God will be lost.

The third text is 1 Peter 1:2. "Chosen and destined [elect according to the foreknowledge of God, KJV] by God the Father and sanctified by the Spirit." Those chosen are the "exiles of the Dispersion" mentioned in the previous verse. God has elected these to salvation.

It is the same in Romans 8:28-30. Persons are foreknown, and the result is their predestination to an effectual calling, justification and glorification. Pink asks,

> In view of these passages (and there are no more) what scriptural ground is there for anyone saying God "foreknew" the acts of certain ones, viz., their "repenting and believing," and that because of those acts he elected them unto salvation? The answer is, None whatever. Scripture never speaks of repentance and faith as being foreseen or foreknown by God. Truly, he did know from all eternity that certain ones would repent and believe, yet this is not what Scripture refers to as the object of God's "foreknowledge." . . . God

foreknows what will be because he has decreed what shall be. It is therefore a reversing of the order of Scripture, a putting of the cart before the horse, to affirm that God elects because he foreknows people. The truth is, he "foreknows" because he has elected.[2]

God's Call

God's eternal, electing purpose to save to himself a people chosen out of all nations does not remain in eternity past. It also has a present expression as described in Romans 8:30, "And those whom he predestined he also called." In theology the call of God is usually termed an "effectual call" to distinguish it from a human call which might or might not be effective. The situation here is quite parallel to that involving the word *foreknow*. On the human level *foreknow* means advance knowledge, while in God's case, where time references do not enter in, it means elective favor or choice. Similarly, *to call* on the human level may make something possible, but it does not actually bring it about. By contrast, in God's case it does.

Take, as an example, a summons to appear in court. A summons is a form of call, a serious one at that. It has the authority of the law and the power of the state behind it. Yet even this extremely serious call does not actually have the power to bring the person summoned to court. She or he may hide from the law, jump bail, skip the country or otherwise thwart the court's intention. Not so with God. In God's case the call actually brings about the response of the one summoned.

Many verses show this meaning of the word but none more clearly than those in Romans 8. John Murray writes, "Nothing clinches the argument for this feature of the call more clearly than the teaching of Romans 8:28-30 where the call is stated to be according to God's purpose and finds its place in the center of that unbreakable chain of events which has its beginning in the divine foreknowledge and its consummation in glorification. This is just saying that the effectual call insures perseverance because it is grounded in the security of God's purpose and grace."[3] Those who have been chosen by God and brought to faith in Christ by the power of this summons are those "called to belong to Jesus Christ" (Rom. 1:6). They are "called to be saints" (Rom. 1:7), that is, to be set apart to God by his call. They are to live holy lives. This is the point of Paul's admonition to the believers in Ephesus, "I therefore, a prisoner for the Lord, beg you to lead a life worthy of the calling to which you have been called" (Eph. 4:1).

Lazarus was dead before Christ called him from the tomb. He was impervious to any call. If you or I were present, we could have called loudly, persuasively and eloquently, but Lazarus would still not have responded. When Jesus called, it was different. His call had power to bring the dead to life. In the same way his call quickens those who have been chosen by God to be his people. And none fail to be quickened! As Jesus said, "My sheep hear my voice, and I know them, and they follow me" (Jn. 10:27).

A Practical Doctrine

Some people believe that election is a useless doctrine and perhaps even pernicious. They say it encourages irresponsibility or even sin. Actually it does nothing of the sort. People are responsible before God for what they do, regardless of whether God elects them to salvation or not. (See *The Sovereign God,* pp. 199-202.) They are not judged by God for failing to do what they cannot do but for failing to do the good they can do and for committing evil which they do not need to do. God forbids such conduct and has established laws of cause and effect to hinder it (Rom. 1:24-32). Election does not affect these facts one way or the other. On the positive side, there are great benefits for Christians.

First, it eliminates boasting within Christian ranks. Non-Christians or those who do not understand election often suppose the opposite, and those who believe in election do sometimes appear smug. But this is a travesty. God tells us explicitly that he has chosen to save a people to himself by grace entirely apart from any merit or receptivity in them, precisely so that pride will be eliminated: "For by grace you have been saved through faith; and this is not your own doing, it is the gift of God—not because of works, lest any man should boast" (Eph. 2:8-9). Salvation is of grace so that the glory might be God's.

Second, this doctrine encourages love for God. If we have a part in salvation, then our love for God is diminished by just that amount. If it is all of God, then our love for him must be boundless. We did not seek him; he sought us. When he sought us, we ran from him. When he came to us in the person of his Son, we killed him. Yet still he came; still he elected a great number of recalcitrant rebels to salvation. "God shows his love for us in that while we were yet sinners Christ died for us" (Rom. 5:8).

Finally, the doctrine of election has this benefit also: it encourages us in evangelism. It is often thought to do the opposite. If God is going to save certain individuals, then he will save them, and there is no point in having anything to do with it. But it does not work that way. God's election does not exclude the use of means through which he calls, and the Bible explicitly tells us that the proclamation of the gospel by believers is that means (1 Cor. 1:21; see Rom. 1:16-17). Moreover, it is only this that gives us hope of success as we proclaim the gospel. If the heart of a sinner is as hard and as opposed to God and his ways as the Bible declares it to be, and if God does not elect the individual, then what hope could we possibly have in witnessing? If God cannot call effectively, then certainly we cannot. But if he is doing such a work in the world, then we can go boldly knowing that all whom God has determined to save will come to him. We do not know who they are. The only way we know the elect is through their response to the gospel and their living of the Christian life which follows that call. But we can call them boldly, knowing that that those who are called by God will surely come.

18 THE KEEPING POWER OF GOD

"There are two points in religion on which the teaching of the Bible is very plain and distinct. One of these points is the fearful danger of the ungodly; the other is the perfect safety of the righteous. One is the happiness of those who are converted; the other is the misery of those who are unconverted. One is the blessedness of being in the way to heaven; the other is the wretchedness of being in the way to hell."[1]

These words by England's Bishop Ryle, introduce the subject of God's perseverance with his saints and tie this chapter to the last. The doctrine of perseverance means that God who has begun a good work in electing and then calling an individual to salvation, according to his own good purpose, will certainly keep on in that purpose until the person elected and called is brought home to the blessedness that has been prepared for him or her. If a person could be saved and then lost, there would be no blessedness in salvation, only anxiety. There could be no safety or happiness. But because God is doing the work and because it is God's nature to finish what he starts, there can be perfect joy for the one who trusts him.

Perseverance is the fifth of the five distinguishing points of Calvinism. It is linked to the other points and gets its strength from them. These have sometimes been used in an acrostic, TULIP, though the words suggested by those letters are not necessarily the best expressions of the doctrines. *T* stands for total depravity, the doctrine that the unregenerate can never do anything to satisfy God's standards of righteousness and, in fact, do not even try. *U* stands for unconditional election, the doctrine considered in the last chapter. It means that salvation begins with God's choice of us and not our choice of God. *L* stands for limited atonement, the doctrine that Christ's death was a real atonement for the specific sins of his people as a result of which they are truly saved. It was not merely a general atonement that makes salvation possible but actually saves no one. *I* stands for irresistible grace, the doctrine which we have referred to in the preceding chapter as effectual calling. Finally, *P* stands for the perseverance of the saints. None of those called by God and redeemed by the Lord Jesus Christ will be lost. As God stands at the beginning and middle of this plan of salvation, so does he stand at the end.

These doctrines were not invented by Calvin, nor were they characteristic of his thought alone during the Reformation period. These are biblical truths taught by Jesus and confirmed by Paul, Peter and all the other Old and New Testament writers. Augustine defended these doctrines against the denials of Pelagius. Luther believed them. So did Zwingli. That is, they believed what Calvin believed and later systematized in his influential *Institutes of the Christian Religion*. The Puritans were Calvinists; it was through them and their teaching that both England and Scotland experienced the greatest and most pervasive national revivals the world has ever seen. In that number were the heirs of John Knox: Thomas Cartwright, Richard Sibbes, Richard Baxter, Matthew Henry, John Owen and others. In America others were influenced by men such as Jonathan Edwards, Cotton Mather and, later, George Whitefield.

In more recent times the modern missionary movement received nearly all its initial impetus and direction from those in the Calvinistic tradition. The list includes William Carey, John Ryland, Henry Martyn, Robert Moffat, David Livingstone, John G. Paton, John R. Mott and others. For all these the doctrines of grace were not an appendage to Christian thought but were rather central, firing and forming their preaching and missionary efforts.

Danger, Sin and Half Belief
Before looking at the biblical teaching regarding perseverance, let us consider what the doctrine is not. First, perseverance does not mean that Christians are free of all spiritual danger just because they are Christians. On the contrary, their danger is even greater, for the world and devil will be active opponents for them.

Consider Christ's prayer for his disciples before his crucifixion. "And now I am no more in the world, but they are in the world, and I am coming to thee. Holy Father, keep them in thy name, which thou hast given me, that they may be one, even as we are one. . . . I have given them thy word; and the world has hated them because they are not of the world, even as I am not of the world. I do not pray that thou shouldst take them out of the world, but that thou shouldst keep them from the evil one" (Jn. 17:11, 14-15). These words are ominous in the context of John's Gospel, for "the evil one" was even then entering into Judas, and "the world" was to condemn Christ to death before morning. This was the deadly environment in which the disciples were to be left. Left to themselves they would surely perish. But Christ prays for them. Although their danger is great, they are to be kept by God's power.

Second, perseverance does not mean that Christians are

free from falling into sin just because they are Christians. We might reason this way on the basis of Christ's prayer in John 17, but this would be wrong; for those for whom Christ prays do sin, though they do not sin so as to fall away from Christ forever. The Lord told Peter, as an example, that he would sin even to the point of denying Christ and that he would do so repeatedly (Jn. 13:38). "Simon, Simon, behold, Satan demanded to have you, that he might sift you like wheat." But Christ added, "I have prayed for you that your faith may not fail; and when you have turned again, strengthen your brethren" (Lk. 22:31-32). In this incident Jesus foretold Peter's denial, but he also foretold his recovery. He assured Peter of his intercession that Peter's faith might not fail.

Noah fell into drunkenness. Abraham lied twice about his wife Sarah, saying she was his sister and thus risking her honor to save his own skin. Lot chose Sodom. Jacob cheated his brother Esau and deceived his father Isaac. David committed adultery with Bathsheba and then tried to cover it up by having her husband, Uriah, killed. In Gethsemane the disciples abandoned Jesus to protect their own lives. Paul and Barnabas fought over John Mark and had to part company. Paul persisted in returning to Jerusalem with the offering from the Gentiles when even the Lord himself appeared to him and forbade him to do it. All these sinned. Yet they were not lost. In fact, there is not a single story in the whole Bible of one who was truly a child of God who was lost. Many were overtaken by sin, but none perished.

Third, perseverance does not mean that those who merely profess Christ without being born again are secure. Specific warnings are given to those who heard the gospel and appeared to trust in Christ, and yet were not truly saved. For example, Jesus said, "If you continue in my word, you are truly my disciples" (Jn. 8:31). This seems to say that perseverance on the part of the believer is the final proof of whether he or she is truly born again. Again, our Lord said,

"He who endures to the end will be saved" (Mt. 10:22). Peter wrote, "Therefore, brethren, be the more zealous to confirm your call and election" (2 Pet. 1:10). It is possible to be quite close to Christian things and yet not truly be regenerate.

The Keeper of Israel

Perseverance in grace means rather, as Thomas Watson puts it, that "the heavenly inheritance is kept for the saints, and they are kept for the inheritance.... Though the saints may come to that pass that they have but little faith, yet not to have no faith. Though their grace may be drawn low, yet it is not drawn dry; though grace may be abated, it is not abolished; though the wise virgins slumbered, yet their lamps were not quite gone out."[2] Perseverance means that once one is in the family of God he or she is always in that family.

The Bible is clear that those who are justified from sin cannot be lost. David wrote in Psalm 138, "The LORD will fulfil his purpose for me; thy steadfast love, O Lord, endures for ever" (v. 8). The author of Hebrews declares, "For by a single offering he [Jesus] has perfected for all time those who are sanctified" (10:14). Paul wrote, "We are afflicted in every way, but not crushed; perplexed, but not driven to despair; persecuted, but not forsaken; struck down, but not destroyed; ... knowing that he who raised the Lord Jesus will raise us also with Jesus and bring us with you into his presence" (2 Cor. 4:8-9, 14). Perseverance is suggested by the images that the Bible applies to believers: trees that do not wither (Ps. 1:3); the cedars of Lebanon that flourish from year to year like California redwoods (Ps. 92:12); a house built upon a rock (Mt. 7: 24); Mount Zion that cannot be moved (Ps. 125:1).

The Old Testament often speaks specifically of the keeping power of God. In Psalm 121 the Lord is compared to a divine watchman whose concern is to keep watch over his people during their earthly lives. The words *keep* or *keeper* are used six times. "He will not let your foot be moved, he who keeps you will not slumber. Behold, he who keeps Israel will neither slumber nor sleep. The LORD is your keeper; the LORD is your shade on your right hand. The sun shall not smite you by day, nor the moon by night. The LORD will keep you from all evil; he will keep your life. The LORD will keep your going out and your coming in from this time forth and for evermore" (vv. 3-8).

Another important passage is Ezekiel 34:11-16. God has been speaking against those who had been the shepherds of Israel who, he says, had not done their work. They were to watch over the sheep, but they had forsaken them. Now, says God, he will do what these faithless leaders had failed to do.

Behold, I, I myself will search for my sheep, and will seek them out. As a shepherd seeks out his flock when some of his sheep have been scattered abroad, so will I seek out my sheep; and I will rescue them from all places where they have been scattered on a day of clouds and thick darkness. And I will bring them out from the peoples, and gather them from the countries, and will bring them into their own land; and I will feed them on the mountains of Israel, by the fountains, and in all the inhabited places of the country. I will feed them with good pasture, and upon the mountain heights of Israel shall be their pasture; there they shall lie down in good grazing land, and on fat pasture they shall feed on the mountains of Israel. I myself will be the shepherd of my sheep, and I will make them lie down, says the Lord GOD. I will seek the lost, and I will bring back the strayed, and I will bind up the crippled, and I will strengthen the weak, and the fat and the strong I will watch over; I will feed them in justice.

In Isaiah 27 God is compared to a keeper of vineyards. "A pleasant vineyard, sing of it! I, the LORD, am its keeper; every moment I water it. Lest any one harm it, I guard it night and day" (vv. 2-3).

Christ drew on these images in his teaching. He compared both himself and the Father to a watchman, shepherd and husbandman to encourage the disciples. The danger was

great without and great within. The disciples possessed an
old nature which would surely drag them down into sin again
and again. But he proclaimed that there was One who was
even greater than the danger and who would certainly pre-
serve them as he had kept and preserved Israel.

Clinching the Nail
In the New Testament there are four great texts which, more
than any others, teach the security of the believer. Two are
from the lips of Jesus. Two are from Paul.

The first is John 6:37-40. "All that the Father gives me will
come to me; and him who comes to me I will not cast out. For
I have come down from heaven, not to do my own will, but
the will of him who sent me; and this is the will of him who
sent me, that I should lose nothing of all that he has given me,
but raise it up at the last day. For this is the will of my Father,
that every one who sees the Son and believes in him should
have eternal life; and I will raise him up at the last day." Having declared that all who have been given to him by the Father
will in fact come to him, the Lord goes on to stress that he will
certainly keep the ones who do come. In Greek this sentence
contains a double negative which might be translated "and
him who comes to me I will never, never cast out."

If the passage stopped at this point, it might be argued that
the double negative refers only to Christ's receiving the one
who comes to him initially—that he will never, never reject
anyone who comes to him—but that such a person may nevertheless decide to leave Christ on his own initiative. But that is
not possible. As Christ makes clear in the following verses, all
who have been given to him by the Father and who therefore
come to him and are received by him will all be raise up at
the last day. He will lose nothing of all that God has g en to
him.

The second great text on perseverance is John 10:27-30,
which follows the same outline as the verses in John 6. But in

214 Awakening to God

this case the Lord is responding to a request from his listeners to speak "plainly." Of course, the difficulty was not in his speech but in their hearing. Nevertheless, he replied, "My sheep hear my voice, and I know them, and they follow me; and I give them eternal life, and they shall never perish, and no one shall snatch them out of my hand. My Father, who has given them to me, is greater than all, and no one is able to snatch them out of the Father's hand" (vv. 27-29). Election, the effectual call and perseverance!

"I know that no one shall ever pluck us out of Christ's hand," says one. "But suppose they choose to jump out of their own accord?"

"They shall never perish," say Jesus.

"What! Never?"

"Never," says Jesus. "They shall never perish, and no one shall snatch them out of my hand."

I have sometimes thought that what Jesus did in uttering these words was like something a carpenter often does. Sometimes in rough carpentry a workman will drive a long nail through thinner boards so that the point sticks out the back. Then with a blow of his hammer he will drive the point of the nail sideways, embedding it in the wood. This is called clinching the nail. It makes the joint just a bit more firm because the nail cannot work itself out from this position.

This is what Jesus did in these verses. He was so interested in getting the doctrine to stick in his disciples' minds that he not only drove one nail, he drove two and clinched them both.

First, he taught that those who are his have been given eternal life. "I give unto them eternal life"—that is the nail. This alone makes the truth fast; for eternal life is life which can never be lost. If it could be lost after a few years or even after many years, it would not be eternal. Nevertheless, Jesus knew that many would attempt to explain it away. So he said, "They shall never perish"—that is the clinch by which the doctrine of perseverance is made fast.

One nail, however well fastened, does not always make a good joint, though. So Jesus went on to drive a second nail and clinch that as well. His second nail, "No one shall snatch them out of my hand." The clincher, "My Father, who has given them to me, is greater than all, and no one is able to snatch them out of the Father's hand."

We can imagine ourselves to be a coin folded in his fingers. That is a secure position for any object but especially for us, considering whose hand holds us. But Jesus adds that the hand of God is over his hand. We are enclosed in two hands. We are doubly secure. If we feel insecure, we can remember that even when we are held in that manner, the Father and Son still have two hands free to defend us.

The third important text on perseverance is from Paul, Romans 8:33-39. It is a sequel to the verses studied in the last chapter and is part of the same sequence of God's acts in salvation which they introduce.

Who shall bring any charge against God's elect? It is God who justifies; who is to condemn? Is it Christ Jesus, who died, yes, who was raised from the dead, who is at the right hand of God, who indeed intercedes for us? Who shall separate us from the love of Christ? Shall tribulation, or distress, or persecution, or famine, or nakedness, or peril, or sword? As it is written, "For thy sake we are being killed all the day long; we are regarded as sheep to be slaughtered." No, in all these things we are more than conquerors through him who loved us. For I am sure that neither death, nor life, nor angels, nor principalities, nor things present, nor things to come, nor powers, nor height, nor depth, nor anything else in all creation, will be able to separate us from the love of God in Christ Jesus our Lord.

Paul lists three possible causes of separation from God's love in these verses but then dismisses them all. First, sin (vv. 33-34). Christians know that although they are justified by God, they are still sinners and sin daily in thought, word and deed.

"Well, what of it?" asks Paul. "Christ has died for sin [past tense]; therefore, in God's sight our sin is gone forever." Suppose someone should accuse us? "God is the judge," Paul answers. Christians have been acquitted before the bench of the highest court of all, and no one is authorized to reopen their case.

Second, in verses 35-37 Paul speaks of suffering, external suffering (tribulation, famine, nakedness, peril) and internal suffering (the anguish of soul known by those who face persecution for the sake of their testimony). This suffering is real. It should be expected, as Paul indicates by his quotation of Psalm 44:22 in 8:36. But suffering will not triumph. It cannot separate us from God's love.

The third potential cause of separation from Christ's love is the existence of supernatural powers (vv. 38-39), but Paul says that even these cannot triumph. Paul knew the extent of spiritual wickedness in this world and had wrestled against it himself. He had written to the Ephesians, "For we are not contending against flesh and blood, but against the principalities, against the powers, against the world rulers of this present darkness, against the spiritual hosts of wickedness in the heavenly places" (6:12). But frightening as these may be, they cannot triumph for the simple reason that Jesus has been victorious over them. To the Colossians Paul wrote, "He disarmed the principalities and powers and made a public example of them, triumphing over them in [Christ]" (2:15).

Saved on Purpose

The final text is Philippians 1:6, which says, "And I am sure that he who began a good work in you will bring it to completion at the day of Jesus Christ." This is a condensed statement of the principle stated at greater length in other places—God finishes what he starts—but it suggests another thought too. Literally, the Greek says that God will "keep on perfecting his work until the day of Christ." To put it in stark language, he will do so whether we want him to or not.

The verse speaks of "a good work" which God will bring to completion. What is that good work? It is not spelled out very clearly in Philippians 1:6 but is in Romans 8:29. "For those whom he foreknew he also predestined to be conformed to the image of his Son." Is this something that is to happen in heaven only? Not at all! It is also God's plan for us now. Philippians 1:6 is saying that God will not give up in his efforts to make us like Christ even now, though we may want him to. Christ is the holy One of God, so this plan involves our growth in holiness. We know that we sin as Christians. What happens when we sin? Does God ignore it? We might like him to, for we sometimes enjoy sin—at least for the moment. But God does not permit us to continue on our way unhindered. He disciplines us for it. He prods us, woos us, sometimes even makes our lives miserable so that we will get out of the path of destruction and back onto the road that he has mapped out for us. Sometimes God will break a Christian's life in pieces if that is what is necessary to get him or her out of sin and back into fellowship.

That is why the doctrine of perseverance is not the dangerous doctrine some have imagined it to be. "Perseverance may be true," says one, "but surely to teach it is dangerous. If people believe that nothing can ever snatch us from God's hand, then surely they will feel free to sin. The doctrine will encourage loose living." The knowledge of the greatness of the love of God which perseveres with us actually tends to keep us faithful. To know such love is to wish, above everything else, not to do anything against it.

Beyond this, knowledge of God's perseverance teaches us to persevere. Our work is often discouraging. We often see few results. But we will keep at it because God has given it to us, and we must be like him in faithfully fulfilling this responsibility. We often find witnessing disheartening. People do not want the gospel. They hate the God who gave it. Still, we will keep at it, knowing that the same God who is able to keep us in the world is able as well to save others out of it. Our families are a special area of responsibility. We are often depressed when a son or daughter or brother or sister or spouse will not walk in God's way. Sometimes the situation seems hopeless. But God does not allow it to be hopeless for us. We will not give up. We will not quit. God is faithful. He is our keeper. With God all things are possible.

We live in a day that is so weak in its proclamation of Christian doctrine that even many Christians cannot see why such truths should be preached or how they can be used of the Lord to save sinners. This was not always so. God used the doctrine of perseverance to save Charles Spurgeon, one of the greatest preachers who ever lived. When he was only fifteen he had noticed how friends of his, who had begun life well, made a wreck of their lives by falling into gross vices. Spurgeon feared that he himself might fall into them. "Whatever good resolutions I might make," he thought, "the probabilities are that they will be good for nothing when temptation actually assails me. I will be like those of whom it is said, 'They see the devil's hook and yet cannot help nibbling at his bait.' I will disgrace myself, and I will be lost." It was then that he heard that Christ will keep his saints from falling. It had a particular charm for him and he found himself saying, "I will turn to Jesus and receive from him a new heart and a right spirit; and so I shall be secured against those temptations into which others have fallen. I shall be preserved by him." It was this truth along with others that brought Spurgeon to the Savior.

Christianity does not have a shaky foundation. It is not a gospel of percentages and possibilities. It is a certain gospel. It is the message of our complete ruin in sin but of God's perfect and certain remedy in Christ.

NOTES

Chapter 1

[1]William James, *The Varieties of Religious Experience* (New York: The New American Library, n.d.).

[2]Harold O. J. Brown, "The Conservative Option," in *Tensions in Contemporary Theology*, ed. Stanley N. Gundry and Alan F. Johnson (Chicago: Moody, 1976), p. 356.

[3]John Calvin, *Institutes of the Christian Religion*, Vol. I, ed. John T. McNeill, trans. Ford Lewis Battles (Philadelphia: Westminster, 1960), 537.

[4]Reuben A. Torrey, *The Person and Work of the Holy Spirit* (1910; rpt. Grand Rapids, Mich.: Zondervan, 1970), pp. 8-9.

[5]See *The Sovereign God* (Downers Grove, Il.: InterVarsity Press, 1978), pp. 137-47.

[6]The points are suggested by George Smeaton, *The Doctrine of the Holy Spirit* (1882; rpt. London: Banner of Truth Trust, 1974), p. 109.

[7]J. I. Packer, *Knowing God* (Downers Grove, Ill.: InterVarsity Press, 1973), p. 63.

Chapter 2

[1]William Barclay, *Flesh and Spirit: An Examination of Galatians 5:19-23* (Nashville: Abingdon, 1962), p. 127.

Chapter 3

[1]Donald Grey Barnhouse, *God's Freedom*, Vol. VI of The Epistle to the Romans, (Grand Rapids, Mich.: Eerdmans, 1958), 35.

[2]John Murray, *Redemption Accomplished and Applied* (Grand Rapids, Mich.: Eerdmans, 1955), p. 164.

[3]John R. W. Stott, *The Baptism and Fullness of the Holy Spirit* (Downers Grove, Ill.: InterVarsity Press, 1964), p. 28.

[4]Charles E. Hummel, *Fire in the Fireplace: Contemporary Charismatic Renewal* (Downers Grove, Ill.: InterVarsity Press, 1978), p. 182.

[5]Parts of these first three chapters are based on earlier studies of the person and work of the Holy Spirit appearing in *The Gospel of John*, Vol. IV (Grand Rapids, Mich.: Zondervan, 1978), pp. 161-92, 209-16, 287-301. See also "The Baptism of the Holy Spirit," *The Gospel of John*, Vol. I, pp. 169-75.

Chapter 4

[1]Murray, p. 79.

[2]For a fuller discussion of the relationship between these various acts and processes, see Murray, pp. 79-87.

[3]William Barclay is one who holds this view. See his *Gospel of John*, Vol. I (Philadelphia: Westminster, 1956), p. 119.

[4]Kenneth S. Wuest, "Great Truths to Live By" in *Wuest's Word Studies from the Greek New Testament*, Vol. III, Part 3, (Grand Rapids, Mich.: Eerdmans, 1966), pp. 55-57.

[5]See James Montgomery Boice, *The Gospel of John*, Vol. I, pp. 93-100, 241-48.

Chapter 5

[1]Norman Vincent Peale, *The Power of Positive Thinking* (New York: Prentice-Hall, 1952), p. 99.

[2]John R. W. Stott, *Your Mind Matters* (Downers Grove, Ill.: InterVarsity Press, 1972), pp. 35-36.

[3]Calvin, pp. 542-92.

[4]Ibid., p. 551.

[5]Leon Morris, *The Gospel According to John* (Grand Rapids, Mich.: Eerdmans 1971), p. 698.

[6]The controversy between Augustine and Pelagius is discussed more fully in volume II of this series, *God the Redeemer* (Downers Grove, Ill.: InterVarsity Press, 1978), pp. 42-44.

[7]Calvin, pp. 583-84.

[8]Ibid., p. 553.

Chapter 6

[1]Martin Luther, *What Luther Says: An Anthology*, Vol. II, pp. 702-04, 715.

[2]Calvin, p. 726.

[3]Thomas Watson, *A Body of Divinity* (1692; rpt. London: Banner of Truth Trust, 1970), p. 226.

[4]Murray, p. 118.

[5]See *God the Redeemer*, pp. 195-202.

[6]Leon Morris, *The Apostolic Preaching of the Cross* (Grand Rapids, Mich.: Eerdmans, 1956), p. 260. Morris has an extended discussion of the justification terminology in the Old and New Testaments (pp. 224-74).

Chapter 7

[1]Calvin, p. 798.

[2]The discussion of Galatians in the previous two sections follows closely sections of my commentary "Galatians" in *The Expositor's Bible Commentary*, ed. Frank Gaebelein (Grand Rapids, Mich.: Zondervan, 1976), Vol. 10, pp. 407-508.

Chapter 8

[1]John R. W. Stott, *The Epistles of John* in the Tyndale New Testament Commentary series (Grand Rapids, Mich.: Eerdmans, 1964), p. 182.

[2]Archibald Alexander, *Thoughts on Religious Experience* (1844; rpt. London: Banner of Truth Trust, 1967), p. 64.

[3]John Calvin, *The Gospel According to St. John 11–21 and The First Epistle of John*, trans. T. H. L. Parker (Grand Rapids, Mich.: Eerdmans, 1961), pp. 259-60.

[4]C. H. Dodd, *The Johannine Epistles* (London: Hodder and Stoughton, 1946), p. 32.

[5]Francis A. Schaeffer, *The Church at the End of the 20th Century* (Downers Grove, Ill.: InterVarsity Press, 1970), p. 145.

Chapter 9

[1]Paul Tournier, *A Place for You* (New York: Harper and Row, 1968), p. 9. The story is told in full on the following pages.

[2]Ibid., p. 12.

[3]Saint Augustine, *The Confessions*, I, 1 in *Basic Writings of Saint Augustine*, ed. Whitney J. Oates (New York: Random House, 1948), Vol. I, p. 3.

[4]Murray, p. 132.

[5]Ibid., pp. 132-33.

[6]John White, *The Fight* (Downers Grove, Ill.: InterVarsity Press, 1976), pp. 129-30.

[7]Ernst Loymeyer, *"Our Father,"* trans. John Bowden (New York: Harper and Row, 1965); Joachim Jeremias, "Abba," in *The Central Message of the New Testament* (London: SCM Press, 1965), pp. 9-30; and Joachim Jeremias, *The Lord's Prayer*, trans. John Reumann (Philadelphia: Fortress, 1964).

[8]Jeremias, *The Lord's Prayer*, p. 19.

[9]*Berakoth* 40a; *Sanhedrin* 70b.

Chapter 10
[1]Murray, pp. 144-45.
[2]Ibid., p. 145.
[3]White, p. 194.
[4]Luther, p. 429.
[5]Donald Grey Barnhouse, *God's Methods for Holy Living* (Grand Rapids, Mich.: Eerdmans, 1951), p. 37.
[6]R. A. Torrey, *The Power of Prayer* (Grand Rapids, Mich.: Zondervan, 1955), p. 77.

Chapter 11
[1]Calvin, *Institutes*, p. 690.
[2]Compare Mt. 10:34-39; Mk. 8:34-38; 10:21, 29-31; Lk. 9:23-25; 14: 26-27, 33; Jn. 12:24-26. Other New Testament writers also make the same point: Paul in Rom. 6:3-11; Gal. 2:20; 6:14 and the author of Hebrews in 12:1-2.
[3]Francis A. Schaeffer, *True Spirituality* (Wheaton, Ill.: Tyndale, 1971), p. 19.
[4]Sherwood Eliot Wirt, *Love Song: Augustine's Confessions for Modern Man* (New York: Harper and Row, 1971), pp. 108-9.
[5]Thomas à Kempis, *Imitation of Christ*, III, 15, 59 (c. 1427; rpt. Chicago: Moody, 1958), pp. 125, 213.

Chapter 12
[1]Roger R. Nicole, "Freedom and Law," *Tenth*, July 1976, p. 23.
[2]Reinhold Niebuhr, *The Nature and Destiny of Man*, one-volume edition of the Gifford Lectures on "Human Nature" and "Human Destiny" (New York: Scribner's, 1949), pp. 54-92.
[3]Ibid., pp. 91-92.
[4]Nicole, pp. 27-28.
[5]Calvin stresses this in his *Institutes*, pp. 834-36.
[6]Ibid., p. 839.

Chapter 13
[1]R. C. Sproul, "Discerning the Will of God," in *Our Sovereign God*, ed. James M. Boice (Grand Rapids, Mich.: Baker, 1977), pp. 106-7.
[2]Some of the material in this chapter has been borrowed from "How to Know the Will of God" and "How to Know the Will of God in Doubtful Situations" in my *How To Really Live It Up* (Grand Rapids, Mich.: Zondervan, 1973), pp. 38-56.
[3]White, p. 154.

Chapter 14
[1]R. A. Torrey, *How To Pray* (Westwood, N. J.: Revell, 1900), pp. 7-31. A more comprehensive book by Torrey is *The Power of Prayer*. Those

who wish to pursue a study of prayer further than this chapter permits may consult Jacques Ellul, *Prayer and Modern Man*, trans. C. Edward Hopkin (New York: Seabury, 1973); O. Hallesby, *Prayer*, trans. Clarence J. Carlsen (Minneapolis: Augsburg, 1960); Andrew Murray, *With Christ in the School of Prayer* (Westwood, N. J.: Revell, 1967); and Calvin, *Institutes*, Vol. II, pp. 850-920.

[2]Calvin, *Institutes*, p. 853.

[3]Ibid., p. 851.

[4]Ibid., p. 850.

[5]Torrey, *The Power of Prayer*, p. 76.

[6]Calvin writes, "Since he [Christ] is the only way, and the one access, by which it is granted us to come to God (cf. John 14:6), to those who turn aside from this way and forsake this access, no way and no access to God remain; nothing is left in this throne but wrath, judgment, and terror. Moreover, since the Father has sealed him (cf. John 6:27) as our Head (Matt. 2:6) and Leader (1 Cor. 11:3; Eph. 1:22; 4:15; 5:23; Col. 1:18), those who in any way turn aside or incline away from him are trying their level best to destroy and disfigure the mark imprinted by God. Thus Christ is constituted the only Mediator, by whose intercession the Father is for us rendered gracious and easily entreated" (*Institutes*, p. 876).

[7]O. Hallesby, *Prayer*, trans. Clarence J. Carlsen (1931; rpt. Minneapolis: Augsburg, 1960), pp. 131-32.

[8]I have written on prayer at greater length in a number of my other books, and sections of the preceding chapter are based upon them. See *Philippians: An Expositional Commentary* (Grand Rapids, Mich.: Zondervan, 1971), pp. 273-79; rpt. "Is Prayer a Problem?" (Philadelphia: Evangelical Foundation, 1974); *The Sermon on the Mount* (Grand Rapids, Mich.: Zondervan, 1972), pp. 183-237; and *How to Really Live It Up*, pp. 20-28.

Chapter 15

[1]Quoted by Reuben A. Torrey, who knew Moody personally, in *How to Succeed in the Christian Life* (Westwood, N. J.: Fleming H. Revell, 1906), p. 49.

[2]John Charles Ryle, *Practical Religion* (1879; rpt. Cambridge: James Clarke & Co., 1959), p. 70.

[3]This movement is discussed at greater length in *The Sovereign God*, pp. 100-1. In recent years there has been a revival of the historical Jesus quest, but along much sounder lines. See James Montgomery Boice, "New Vistas in Historical Jesus Research," *Christianity Today*, 15 March, 1968, pp. 3-6.

[4]Ryle, p. 71. I have discussed the nature of the Bible, its claims about itself and its effects on those who read it, as well as the evidence for its being the Word of God, in *The Sovereign God*, pp. 39-79. Subsequent

chapters discuss inerrancy, modern biblical criticism and the basic principles according to which the Bible should be studied.
[5]Torrey, *How to Succeed,* p. 50.
[6]Ryle, p. 96.
[7]Torrey, *How to Succeed,* p. 60.
[8]Ralph L. Keiper, "The Rewards of Bible Study," in *Why and How to Study the Scriptures* by James Montgomery Boice and Ralph L. Keiper (Philadelphia: Evangelical Ministries, 1977), p. 29.

Chapter 16
[1]Torrey, *How to Succeed,* p. 83.
[2]Helen H. Harris, *The Newly Recovered Apology of Aristides* (London: Hodder and Stoughton, 1893); cited in Sherwood Eliot Wirt, *The Social Conscience of the Evangelical* (New York: Harper and Row, 1968), pp. 29-30.
[3]Calvin, *Institutes,* Vol. I, pp. 790-91.

Chapter 17
[1]Arthur W. Pink, *The Attributes of God* (Grand Rapids, Mich.: Baker, n.d.), p. 20.
[2]Ibid., p. 24.
[3]Murray, p. 91.

Chapter 18
[1]J. C. Ryle, *Old Paths* (1877; rpt. Cambridge: James Clarke & Co., 1977), p. 476.
[2]Watson, pp. 279-80.

James, William, 15
Jeremias, Joachim, 113
Jesus Christ. _See_ Christ
Jesus
John, the apostle, 17,
104, 172
John the Baptist, 43-44,
188, 199
Jonah, 197-98
Joy, 30, 91
Judas, 189
Judgment, 67-68, 74
Justification, 38, 53, 108,
202; a legal term, 73-75
Justification by faith, 71-
91; defined, 72-77;
hinge of salvation, 71-
81; misused, 186-87;
plus works, 83-91
Keeping power of God,
the, 207-18
Kindness, 31
Knowledge, 19; impor-
tance of, 95; means of
grace, 123-24; of God,
100
Knox, John, 208
Laban, 138
Law, 119, 145, 148; con-
demns, 87; purpose of
the, 88; son of the, 89;
temporary, 89
Lazarus, 204
Liberty, 89
Life, 142; by the Spirit,
90-91
Limited atonement, 208
Livingstone, David, 209
Lohmeyer, Ernst, 113
Lord's Prayer, the, 113,
168
Lot, 210
Love, 29-30, 91; for God,
205; practical expres-
sions of, 104-5; test of,
102-5
Luther, Martin, 55, 71,
94, 123, 208; boldness
in prayer, 172-73
Marcion, 99

Mark, John, 172-210
Marriage, 135, 143-44
Mary of Bethany, 104,
189
Mather, Cotton, 209
Martyn, Henry, 209
Medicare, 192
Meekness, 31
Miracles, 19
Moffat, Robert, 209
Moody, Dwight L., 175
Moralists, 77-78
Morris, Leon, 75
Moses, 76, 198; law of, 85
Mott, John R., 209
Murray, John, 10, 39, 52,
72, 109, 119-20, 203
Myconius, Frederick,
172-73
Mythologies, 26
Naturalism, 146
Negative principle, the,
131-42
New birth, the, 51-60,
198; divine initiative in,
54-56; means of, 56-59.
See Regeneration,
Rebirth
New commandment, the,
102-3
New morality, 100
Niebuhr, Reinhold, 146
Nietzsche, 146
Noah, 210
Obedience, 184
Objectivity, 15
Old Testament, pre-
pared for Christ's
coming, 26
Options, limited by
Scripture, 157-58
Ordo salutis, 52-53
Owen, John, 208
Packer, J. I., 22
Paradox, 143
Past, rejection of the,
145
Patience, 30
Paton, John G., 209
Paul, 17, 33, 208; and

Barnabas, 210; and
freedom, 148; conver-
sion of, 79-80; life of, 85
Peace, 30, 91
Peale, Norman Vincent,
63
Pelagius, 67, 208
Pentecost, 45-46, 66-67,
190
People, categories of,
77-81
Perfection, 118-20
Perseverance, 10, 197,
207-18; defined, 211-
13; major texts for, 213-
18; what it is not, 209-
11
Person, defined, 18
Peter, 17, 21, 26, 66-68,
85, 101, 190, 208;
Christ's prayer for, 210;
delivered from prison,
171-72
Philip, 17
Poverty, 144
Power, 57
Prayer, 14, 157, 163-73,
187; according to God's
will, 171-73; a problem,
164-66; for believers
only, 169; importance
of, 163-64; in the Holy
Spirit, 170-71; means of
grace, 124-25; privilege
of, 112-15, 163-64;
through Jesus Christ,
169-70; to God the Fa-
ther, 166-69
Predestination, 53, 200
Privileges, family, 112-15
Prophecy, 19
Propitiation, 72-73
Pruning, 32-33
Puritans, the, 208
Questionable matters,
150
Rebirth, 28-29, 37. _See_
New birth, the; Regen-
eration
Redemption, 72-73